A SKETCH

OF THE

NORTHERN BALOCHI LANGUAGE

CONTAINING

A GRAMMAR, VOCABULARY

A SKETCH

OF THE

NORTHERN BALOCHI LANGUAGE

CONTAINING

A GRAMMAR, VOCABULARY

AND

SPECIMENS OF THE LANGUAGE

M. LONGWORTH DAMES

GYAN

Published by

Gyan Publishing House
5, Ansari Road
Daryaganj, New Delhi-110002
Phone: 011-47034999, 9811692060
E-mail: books@gyanbooks.com

Distribution Network
gyanbooks.com
India, USA, Canada, UK, Australia

ISBN: 978-93-6780-222-9 (PB)

First Published, 1881

2nd Impression 2025

Printed at: Gyan Press, Delhi.

A SKETCH OF THE NORTHERN BALOCHI LANGUAGE CONTAINING A GRAMMAR, VOCABULARY
Author: M. LONGWORTH DAMES

A SKETCH

OF THE

NORTHERN BALOCHI

LANGUAGE

CONTAINING

A GRAMMAR, VOCABULARY

AND

SPECIMENS OF THE LANGUAGE

BY

M. LONGWORTH DAMES, C. S.

EXTRA NUMBER TO JOURNAL, ASIATIC SOCIETY, BENGAL, PART I FOR 1880.

CALCUTTA:

PRINTED BY J. W. THOMAS, BAPTIST MISSION PRESS,

PUBLISHED BY THE

ASIATIC SOCIETY, 57, PARK STREET.

1881.

INTRODUCTION.

1. The Balochí language belongs to the Iranian branch of the Aryan family. It is found in two distinct forms; the Northern dialect which is here treated of, and the Southern or Makráni dialect which has been lately dealt with in Major Mockler's Grammar. The Northern dialect is spoken among the Rind Baloches living in the neighbourhood of the Bolán Pass in Kachi, and on the Upper Sindh and South Panjáb frontiers. The tribes speaking this dialect are the Rinds, Dombkís, Maghasís, Jakránís, Marrís, Bugtís, Mazárís, Drishaks, Gorchánís, Lashárís, Durkánís, Leghárís, Hadyánís, Lunds, Khosas, Bozdárs, and Kaisaránís. These tribes come into contact with populations speaking Sindhí, Panjábí, Brahói, and Pashto. The Indian languages, Sindhí and Panjábí, have affected the Balochí Vocabulary considerably, Pashto very slightly if at all, while Brahói has probably borrowed considerably from Balochí. The Brahóis commonly understand Balochí, and it is the commonest medium of communication between them and the Balochí speaking tribes. The best Baloch is probably spoken among the Dombkís and Bugtís, the most corrupt perhaps among the Bozdárs. But the differences in dialect between one tribe and another are very slight, while between the Northern and Southern dialects the difference is so great that the one is almost unintelligible to the tribes speaking the other. The Sarawán and Jahlawán tribes of Brahóis occupy a broad belt of country dividing one dialect from the other.

2. This dialect was first dealt with by Leech in the Journal of the Bengal Asiatic Society for 1840. His sketch was commented on by Lassen in the "Zeitschrift für die Kunde des Morgenlandes" for 1841. Leech gives a small Vocabulary. Gladstone's Bilúchí Manual (Lahore, 1873) and Bruce's Manual (Lahore, 1869) both include Vocabularies, but no attempt has hitherto been made to compile a full or systematical vocabulary. There is a scanty vocabulary of Southern Balochí in Masson's travels, but this dialect is fully dealt with by Major Mockler, and a vocabulary is also promised. The difference between the dialects is so

1

great however that Major Mockler's works are of small value to the student of Northern Balochí, which is of most importance politically speaking. Partly to supply this want, and partly as a contribution to the study of an interesting group of languages, I have compiled this vocabulary, for which I have been collecting words for four years on the Southern Deráját Frontier, and in the Sulaiman Hills, and for a short time in Sibi and Kachí.

3. Balochí is as regards vocabulary a mixed language. The original old Persian stock has formed the nucleus round which the alien elements have gathered. The principal borrowings have been from Sindhí or the South Panjábí dialect which is nearly akin to it. Correspondences are pointed out in the vocabulary, Indian words being generally marked as Sindhí, as that is the source from which they are immediately derived. But by pointing out the correspondence I do not mean to assert that in every case Balochí has borrowed from Sindhí. Sometimes Sindhí may be the borrowing language, and in many cases both languages are indebted to modern Persian or Arabic. Though the numerical proportion of Sindhí words as shown in the vocabulary may seem very large it is not so in actual practice, as many of these words are of rare occurrence, and others only locally used. Nearly all the words in commonest use, especially the verbs, are pure Balochí.

4. I prefix an outline of the grammar of Balochí. Lassen has already treated of the sounds, but the materials furnished him by Leech were too imperfect, and too full of misprints to be a safe foundation to build on in every case. Although, however, he was led astray in individual cases, the true character of the language did not escape him, and the remarks that follow are based on his.

BALOCHI GRAMMAR.

TABLE OF BALOCHI SOUNDS.

	SURD.			SONANT.			Nasal.	Sibilant.	Semi-vowels.	Aspirate.
	Mute.	Aspirate.		Mute.	Aspirate.					
Guttural ...	ک k	کهه kh	خ *kh*	گ g	گهه gh	غ *gh*	ں *n*	...	...	ﮦ h
Palatal ...	چ ch	چهه chh	...	ج j	جهه jh	...	...	ش sh ژ zh	ي y	...
Cerebral ...	ٹ ṭ	ٹهه ṭh	...	ڈ ڑ ḍ ṛ	ڈهه ḍh	...	...	...	...	...
Dental ...	ت t	تهه th	ث *t*	د d	دهه dh	ذ *dh*	ن n	س s ز z	ل l ر r	...
Labial ...	پ p	پهه ph	ف f	ب b	بهه bh	و v, w	م m	...	...	...

THE ALPHABET.

Balochí can hardly be called a written language. It is only within the last few years that Balochís have begun to write it, Persian being the ordinary medium of written communication and the Balochís considering their language to be merely a colloquial form of Persian. In writing, uniformity of spelling is little attended to. As the Persian character is the only one current in the countries where Balochí is spoken, I have employed it in the Vocabulary, giving a transliteration of all words in the Roman character. Short vowels are not marked in the Persian character, as the transliteration renders it unnecessary. The Arabic letters ث and ذ are retained to represent certain Balochí sounds corresponding, or nearly so, with their Arabic values, the representation of these sounds by س and ز being insufficient and misleading. The other Arabic letters ح, ص, ض, ط, ظ, ع, and ق are omitted as unnessary having no distinct value in Balochí. In the borrowed Arabic words phonetic correctness is all that is aimed at. Aspirates are represented by ھ or *h* following the aspirated consonant. The cerebrals are marked as in Urdú.

The Persian Alphabet as applied to Balochí.

Persian.	Roman.	Value.
ا	a, i, u, á, e, ai, o, au	As in Persian, an initial introducing all vowels. With the short vowel marks ـَ ـِ ـُ it forms a, i, u. With *madda* آ it forms á. With ی following it forms í, e, ai. With و following it forms ú, o, au. As a medial and final it is always á.
ب	b	As in English and Persian.
بھ	bh	Aspirated *b*.
پ	p	As in Persian and English.
پھ	ph	Aspirated *p*.
ت	t	Dental *t* as in Persian.
تھ	th	Aspirated *t*.
ث	*th*	As in Arabic, English *th* in *breath, health*.
ٹ	ṭ	Cerebral *ṭ* pronounced as in Hindústání.
ٹھ	ṭh	Aspirated *ṭ*.
ج	j	*J* as in English.
جھ	jh	Aspirated *j*.
چ	ch	As in English *church*.

Persian.	Roman.	Value.
چهه	chh	Aspirated *ch.*
خ	*kh*	An aspirate guttural as in Persian, pronounced without harshness as in Pashto.
د	d	Dental *d* as in Persian.
ده	dh	Aspirated *d.*
ڈ	ḍ	Cerebral *ḍ* as in Hindústání.
ڈه	ḍh	Aspirated *ḍ.*
ذ	*dh*	As in Arabic, or English *th* in *brother*, *breathe.*
ر	r	A clearly trilled *r*, as in Persian.
ڑ	ṛ	Cerebral *ṛ* as in Hindústání, and like it nearly connected in sound with ڈ *ḍ.*
ز	z	As English *z.*
ژ	zh	As in Persian, or *s* in English *measure.*
س	s	As in Persian. English *s.*
ش	sh	As in Persian, the palatal sibilant. English *sh.*
غ	*gh*	As in Persian. A slightly pronounced guttural, not so harsh as in Arabic or Pashto.
ف	f	A pure labial *f*, not partly dental as English *f.*
ک	k	As English *k* without any palatalization as in Persian.
گ	g	*G* hard as in English and Persian without palatalization.
م	m	As English *m.*
ن	n	As English *n.* Also as a slightly pronounced guttural nasal, as in the final *n* of Persian or Hindústání plurals.
و	w, v	Either as English *w* or as a purely labial *v*, not as English *v.*
ه	h	As English *h.* Occasionally mute as a final. When so mute it is not represented in transliterations.
ی	y	As English *y.* Sometimes pronouncd with a slight tendency to become *zh.*

BALOCHI SOUNDS.*

1.—CONSONANTS.

ک k corresponds with Persian k, which however more usually appears in Balochi as کھ kh or خ *kh*.

کھ kh as an initial represents Persian ک k or خ *kh*; e. g.,

Balochi khush-a*gh*	Persian kush-tan
B. khar	P. *kh*ar
B. khan-a*gh*	P. kun

As a final it sometimes represents گ g; e. g.,

B. gwánkh	P. báng
B. gurkh	P. gurg

خ *kh* seldom occurs initially, its place being taken by kh. As a final it corresponds with Persian k or g; e. g.,

B. há*kh*	P. *kh*ák
B. re*kh*	P. reg

گ g corresponds either with Persian g or b. As an initial gw answers to b (original v); e. g.,

B. gandím	P. gandum
B. gíst	P. bíst
B. gwá*th*	P. bád
B. gwaf-a*gh*	P. báftan
B. ge*th*	P. bed

گھ gh does not seem to occur in true Balochi words, but to be confined to words of Indian origin.

غ *gh* hardly ever appears as an initial. As a medial it corresponds with Persian g and h; as a final usually with h (whether pronounced or mute in modern Persian, also occasionally with g; e. g.,

B. ja*gh*ar	P. jigar
B. ni*gh*áh	P. nigáh
B. di*gh*ár	P. díhár
B. jí*gh*	P. zih
B. rosha*gh*	P. rozah
B. ra*gh*	P. rag

In the words sa*gh*ar 'head,' P. sar, and na*gh*an 'bread,' P. nán, the g*h* has no consonant corresponding to it in the Persian.

* These explanations follow the order of sounds in the Table, p. 3.

The *gh* appears to be inherent in past participles, answering to the final h of the Persian, but it is not heard except in compound forms when followed by a vowel. Thus khu*tha*, p. p. of khana*gh* means 'done,' but khu*tha*-*gh*-ant 'they have done.'

ں *n* frequently occurs as a final, in the place of n or nt; e. g.,

khana*gh*en — khana*gh*ant.

Occasionally owing to a nasal style of pronunciation, *n*w stands for m, and *n* is interpolated as a final; e. g.,

nyá*n*wán — nyámá

چ ch generally corresponds with the same letter in Persian.

چھ chh also represents Persian ch; e.g.,

B. chhá*th*	P. cháh
B. chham	P. chashm

ج j corresponds either with original Persian j or z; e.g.,

B. jihán	P. jahán
B. jan	P. zan
B. jí*gh*	P. zih

جھ jh is only found in words of Indian origin.

The cerebral consonants are found almost entirely in words of Indian origin. Before a dental, ر r is occasionally pronounced ڑ ṛ, as maṛd for mard, gaṛtha for gartha; but this is not universal and has not been marked in the Vocabulary. Leech represents this by ḍ, but I have never heard it so pronounced.

ت t represents an original t, which however more usually becomes تھ th.

تھ th as an initial commonly represents an original t. As a final, and after a consonant medially, it often corresponds with Persian d; e.g.,

B. thá*kh*tha	P. tá*kh*ta
B. thafar	P. tabar
B. árth	P. árad
B. khanth	P. kunad
B. burtha	P. burda

ث *th* (pronounced as in Arabic, like English *th* in *nothing*, *heath*), does not occur initially. As a medial and final it corresponds with Persian d. As a final it does not occur, unless preceded by a vowel; e. g.,

B. brá*th*	P. birádar
B. gwá*th*	P. bád
B. ro*th*	P. rúda
B. ro*th*	P. ravad
B. sí*th*	P. súd
B. rasi*tha*	P. rasúda

د d corresponds with Persian d as an initial and occasionally after a consonant; e.g.,

B. dem	P. adîm
B. khanda*gh*	P. *kh*and-údan

ڈھ dh only occurs in words of Indian origin.

ذ *dh* (pronounced like English *th* in *mother*, *breathe*) never occurs initially. As a final and medial it corresponds with Persian d; e. g.,

B. dí*dh*ar	P dídár
B. sa*dh*	P. sad
B. ro*dh*	P. rod

In some verbs *dh* as a characteristic represents a consonant which is lost in modern Persian; e. g.,

B. ru*dh*-a*gh*, p.p. rustha	P. rustan, Imp. rú
B. nyá*dh*-a*gh*	P. nihádan, nih.
B. sho*dh*-a*gh*	P. shustan, shú, p.p. shustha

In ma*dh*a*kh* 'locust' *dh* corresponds with l in Persian mala*kh*.

In ká*gh*a*dh* کاغذ the Persian spelling is preserved, though ذ is pronounced *dh* not z.

In na*dh*ra it represaents Arabic ظ in نظر.

ن n corresponds with Persian n.

پ p corresponds with Persian p, also with f before a consonant; e. g.,

B. hapt	P. haft
B. gwaptha	P. báfta

پھ ph as an initial represents Persian p and f; e. g.,

B. phanch	P. panj
B. phusht	P. pusht
B. phur	P. pur
B. phráh	P. farákh

ف f seldom occurs initially, its place being taken by ph. As a medial and final it commonly represents Persian b; e. g.,

B. thafar	P. tabar
B. shaf	P. shab
B. áf	P. áb

ب b corresponds with Persian b as an initial and when not preceded by a vowel.

بھ bh is found only in words of Indian origin.

و w, v, has two sounds. The most usual is that of English w, which it receives generally when followed by a vowel, and the other that of a labial v (bh in Ellis's palæotype), which it receives when followed by a consonant or as a final, and in borrowed words of Sindhí origin. With both pronunciations it often corresponds with Persian b; e. g.,

B. zawán	P. zabán
B. warná	P. barná
B. savz	P. sabz
B. wháv	P. *kh*wáb

Combined with h, w is pronounced like English wh in *which;* wh and w alone often correspond with Persian *khw* خو or *kh* followed by a labial vowel (u, ú, o). The guttural is either preserved in the aspirate h, or more frequently lost altogether (see h); e. g.,

B. whán	P. *kh*wán
B. whár	P. *kh*wár
B. wash	P. *kh*ush
B. wán-a*gh*	P. *kh*wán-dan
B. war-a*gh*	P. *kh*ur-dan

م m corresponds with Persian m.

س s corresponds with Persian s.

ش sh as an initial corresponds with Persian sh. As a final and medial it corresponds either with sh or z; e. g.,

B. shaf	P. shab
B. ash	P. az
B. namásh	P. namáz
B. seshin	P. sozan
B. rosh	P. roz

Sher 'below' seems to correspond with Persian zer, but there is no other case of initial sh corresponding with z. Sher may be a contraction of ash-er 'from below.'

ز z corresponds either with Persian s or z; e.g.,

B. zuwár	P. suwár

In the following words z corresponds with Persian d; *viz.*,

B. zí	P. dí roz
A. zán-a*gh*	P. dán-istan
B. zámá*th*	P. dámád

In zí 'yesterday,' mazai*n* 'great,' zána*gh* 'know,' and zirde, a poetical word meaning 'heart,' the original Zend z is preserved. In záma*th* z represents an original j.

In zik and zará*gh* z corresponds with the j of Sindhí jik and jaru, but these words may have been borrowed by Sindhí. Cf. Pashto zik.

ژ zh corresponds with Persian sh, z and j; e. g.,

B. duzhman	P. dushman
B. azhmán	P. ásmán
B. drázh	P. daráz
B. wázhá	P. *kh*wája

ي y, و r, and ل l correspond with the same letters in Persian.

ه h generally represents an old Persian h, modern Persian h or *kh*; e. g.,

B. hushk	P. *kh*ushk
B. hon	P. *kh*un
B. hí*kh*	P. *kh*úk
B. phráh	P. farâ*kh*

Borrowed Arabic words beginning with خ undergo a similar change, as:—

B. hair	A. *kh*air
B. hatar	A. *kh*atar

The above noted correspondences may be tabulated as follows:

Persian.		Balochi.
k	as an initial	kh
	medial, final	*kh*
kh	initial	h, kh
	medial	*kh*
	final	h, *kh*
g	initial	g
	medial	*gh*
	final	*gh*, *kh*
ch	initial	chh
t	initial	th
d	medial, final	*th*, *dh*, th
p	initial	ph
f	initial	ph
b	medial, final	f, v, w
sh	medial	zh (occasionally)
s	initial, medial	z, zh (occasionally)
z	initial	j

Persian.		Balochi.
z	medial } final }	sh, zh
h	medial } final }	*gh*
	initial	occasionally omitted

It will be noticed that the aspirates of the surd row (kh, chh, th) are very common, replacing the corresponding unaspirated Persian consonants, while those of the sonant row (gh, jh, dh, bh) seem to be entirely confined to words of Indian and Brahuí origin.

The letters *kh*, *gh*, *th*, *dh*, and f are usually medials or finals, representing the Persian letters, shown in the above table. *Th* and *dh* are never initials, and *kh*, *gh* and f, when they occur in borrowed words of modern introduction as initials, are usually pronounced kh, g and ph.

An initial h is occasionally lost altogether; e. g.,

B. aste*n*	P. hastand
B. am	P. ham

II. VOWELS.

The vowel sounds in Balochi generally agree with those of *Kh*urásání Persian. They may be arranged as follows:—

Long	á, í, ú
Short	a, i, u
Diphthongs	e, ai, o, au

The most noticeable point of difference from Persian is the frequent substitution of the palatal series í, i, e for the labial series ú, u, o; e.g.,

B. sí*th*	P. súd
B. dír	P. dúr
B. seshin	P. sozan
B. gandím	P. gandum
B, bí*th*a	P. búda
B. hí*kh*	P. *kh*úk
B. wasí	P. *kh*usú
B. sírmu*gh*	P. surma

A similar change sometimes affects borrowed Arabic words; e. g.,

B. málím	A. málúm
B. hír	A. húr

In a few cases the change is reversed; e. g.,

B. osht-a*gh*	P. ist-ádan
B. súf	P. sev

Other variations from the Persian vowel system are rare.

THE NOUN.

I—TERMINATIONS.

1. Balochi nouns in their formation correspond closely with Persián. The original terminal vowels have been lost, and the majority of nouns now terminate in consonants. There is no distinction of gender.

2. Vowel-endings.

á. The majority of nouns ending in á are borrowed from Sindhí or Arabic. In the former case á sometimes represents Sindhí o, therein corresponding more nearly with Panjábí; e. g.,

Ar. hayá, duá.

Si. bhá, jheṛá, thorá, trámá, velá.

The words wázhá, zá, chawá, pásná and begá are not borrowed. Of these wázhá (P. khwájah) and begá in inflected forms drop the á, and take the termination ah as a base of inflection; e. g.,

wázhá, pl. wázhahán̲, lords

begá: abl. begahá, in the evening.

The borrowed noun velá time, is similarly treated. Other nouns ending in á take no inflections. Some Sindhi nouns as jheṛá, thorá have an alternative form in o which can be inflected.

í. This is a common termination being commonly used as in Persian to form abstracts as duzí, 'theft' from duz 'thief,' sakí strength from sak 'strong' &c., also as the termination of other abstract nouns not directly formed from Balochí bases as shádhí 'rejoicing,' ziyání 'injury.' It occurs also in other nouns as godí 'lady,' druhání 'pistol,' mavárkí 'assembly,' pahlí 'rib' (P. pahlú). A as a termination of borrowed words í is also found as in chárí 'spy,' mehí 'buffalo,' phallí 'section of a tribe.'

O is of frequent occurrence both in pure Balochí and in borrowed words; e. g.,

Balochi	dí*th*lo,	mist	(P. dúd).
	shá*th*lo,	dove	
	bathlo,	mortar	
	ná*kh*o,	uncle	
	go*kh*o,	span	
	mo*kh*o	spider	
	go	race, prize	
	jo	watercourse	
	gwando	alligator	
	duggo	eagle	
	jaddo	cave	
	phalo	direction	

	surgo	speech	
	leṛo	camel	
Borrowed			
	ḍaḍḍo,	pony	Si. ḍraḍro
	paraḍḍo,	echo	Si. paránḍo
	ghoṛo.	a band of horse	
	shaddo	a turban	
	lekho	reckoning.	

This o nearly corresponds in sound to the close English o, and never has the open Italian sound. Most words ending in o change it to av when followed by a vowel, whether this vowel commences a following word or an inflectional suffix. The o of the first eight words in the above list (dí*th*lo to jo inclusive) does not undergo this change. Go and jo are radical words, and the others end in the syllables lo and *kh*o which probably had originally a distinct force of their own; e. g.,

nákho, jo } form the plural { ná*kh*oá*n*, joá*n*

but phalo, jaddo } are inflected { phalavá, jaddavá.

Ḍíhav 'leopard' may be classed with words ending in o, though I have never heard the termination pronounced otherwise than av. This v is a purely labial sound, not the English v.

Ú. ú as a termination does not seem to occur in pure Balochi words. It is found in a few words of Sindhi origin and undergoes no change in inflections; e. g.,

ánú, an egg
ṭilú, a bell
varú, a beam
límúa, lemon (Arabic).

E has not been met with except in *kahne* 'pigeon,' also pronounced kahní.

Au is only found in *jau* 'barley.'

3. Special terminations.

(*a*). *Verbal Nouns,*

A*gh*. This is the termination of the infinitive, and verbal noun which corresponds with it in form. It apparently corresponds with the Pashto verbal noun in *ah*, as final *gh* in Balochí generally corresponds with Persian h. A*gh* as a termination corresponds with the Persian termination *ah* in many other nouns; e. g., rama*gh* "a flock of goats," áhanja*gh* "a sash" &c. Some are verbal nouns in form as gwánza*gh* "a swing." The termination a*gh* also forms collective nouns as murdána*gh* "the fingers," from murdán, phá*dh*a*gh* "legs," from phá*dh*.

O*kh*. This termination forms the noun of agency from the Verbal base, and may be used with almost any verb; e.g., thurso*kh* "a coward," from thursa*gh* "to fear;" waro*kh* "an eater," from wara*gh*. These nouns of agency can be used and inflected as adjectives; e. g.,

miṛo*kh*, a fighter

miṛo*kh*en̲ bíng, fighting dog.

O*kh* is ocasionally found in other nouns besides those of agency as in ganno*kh* 'fool.'

(*b*) *Abstract Nouns.*

í. This is the commonest termination for abstract nouns, which may be formed from other nouns, or adjectives; e. g., duzí "theft," sakmardi "valour," *gh*amí "grief."

Ádh. Used in forming abstracts from adjectives of dimension; as,

gwandá*dh*, shortness

drázhá*dh*, length

phráhá*dh*, breadth.

útá; as azmútá 'examination' from ázmaina*gh*.

ár; as dídár 'sight,' raftár 'paces.'

(*c*) *Collective Nouns.*

A*gh*. See above under verbal nouns.

gal. This is most usually employed to form collectives; e. g.,

jangal, a band of women from *jan*.

zahgal, a flock of kids from *zah*.

pahar, as gwar-pahar, a flock of lambs.

(*d*) *Diminutives.*

Ak, akh, ikh. This termination is frequently employed to form diminutives, sometimes modifying the base; e. g.,

janikh or jinkh girl, from jan woman

gwarakh lamb, from the base gwar—cf. guránḍ ram, and gwar-papar flock of lambs.

kisánakh very small, from kisáin.

This termination is occasionally used when all diminutive signification has been lost, as wasarikh, "father-in-law," (Persian *kh*usar).

Ro, occasionally used, as in kisánro, a diminutive of kisáin̲ 'small.' Possibly the termination lo in dí*th*lo, shá*th*lo had originally the force of a diminutive. Compare also the adverbs khamro "a very little," from khan, and chíklo "a little."

4. Compound nouns and adjectives.

Compounds are numerous, and may be classed under the Sanskrit divisions of Dwandwa, Tatpurusha, Karmadháraya and Bahuvríhi, or Copulative, Qualifying, Descriptive and Possessive.

a. Copulative. This class consists of nouns inseparably coupled together, only the latter being subject to inflection ; e. g.,

phol-phurs, enquiry
thau*kh*-tawár, conversation
chukh-chorí, children.

b. Qualifying or dependent. In this class the latter member of the compound is qualified by the former. The latter member may be either a noun or a verbal root, the verbal noun in o*kh* being occasionally but not often used ; e. g.,

(1). When both members are nouns.
jogin-dár, a pestal (lit. mortar-stick).
mazár-dumb, a plant (lit. tiger-tail).
rosh-ásán, sunrise.
chagá-hálwar, a matter of jest.
chham-phusht, eyelid.
máh-*gh*umá, eclipse of the moon.

(2.) When the first member is a noun and the latter a verbal root.
shírwár, milk-drinking
rozh-gír, eclipse of the sun (sun-seizing).
go*dh*án̤-din, udder-tearing (name of a plant).
shav-khash, night-expeller (the planet Venus).
mar-khusho*kh*, man-slayer.
sangband, connected by marriage.

c. Descriptive. In this class the first member is an adjectives, numeral or other word simply describing or defining the second ; e. g.,

syah-áf, perennial stream, (lit. blackwater).
drázhdár, a beam (longwood).
má*dh*gor, female wild ass.
ergwá*th*, the leeside (lit. downwind).
chyár-gíst, fourscore.

d. Possessive. These are formed in a similar manner to the last class, with the force of adjectives or descriptive epithets, the possession of the qualities described being implied ; e. g.,

hor-dast, empty-handed.
phásh-phá*dh*, barefoot.
swe*th*-rísh, greybeard
syáh-gwar, black-breast (e. g. the black partridge).
pho*dh*án̤-demí, the name of a flower (lit. thither-faced).
dír-zána*gh*, far-knowing.
dast-bastha*gh*, hands joined.

5. Inflection of nouns.

The suffixes used in forming the different cases are á, ár, e*gh*, á*n*, á*n*rá and ání, but these suffixes are put to a great variety of uses which will be considered under the different cases.

The most usual inflection is that in á. It may be used us an instrumental or nominative with verbs in a past tense, as an accusative, ablative, and locative, its place is to a certain extent taken in the plural by the suffix ání, the use of which is however more restricted.

(1) *The Nominative.* The nominative of all intransitive verbs, and of transitive verbs in the present and future is the simple uninflected noun. With transitive verbs in tenses derived from the past participle the instrumental construction is employed, the inflected form in á being used for the agent while the object is left uninflected.

(2) *Genitive.* In most cases the simple base is used with a genitive signification, but if greater precision is required the suffix e*gh* is used, as Á*n* mard bachh, that man's son; but hawe bachh á*n*hí marde*gh* e*n*, he is the son of that man.

(3) *Dative.* The termination ár or ar is employed for the dative, as: Mardumár na*gh*aná dá*th*a-í, he gave the man bread.

(4) *Accusative.* The most usual ending of the accusative is á, but ár is frequently used, especially when emphasis is required or to distinguish a nearer object from a more remote; e. g., má Balochiyá roṭí-ár na*gh*an khanu*n*. In Balochí we call "roṭí" na*gh*an.

The uninflected noun is also sometimes used for the accusative.

(5) *Ablative, Locative.* The inflected form in á is used with the prepositions go "with," azh "from," pha "on," ma*n* "in," gwar "in possession of," dan "into," and avr "in, upon," which alone precede the noun. It also expresses without a preposition position, motion to or from, time when. The meaning *from* is often implied without the use of the preposition azh; e. g.,

Á*n* ki khái chí ká*dh*irá	Whatever thing comes from God
Bahr-khananí go há*dh*irá	That I will divide with my heart.
Har shákhá házár shá*kh* bí*th*a	On every branch a thousand branches sprang.
Har shá*kh*á wa*th*í gul·bí*th*a.	On every branch its own flower.

Plural.

(6). *Án.* The termination á*n* is used for the nominative and accusative plural, but the singular forms are perhaps more frequently used. With numerals the singular is almost exclusively used.

á*n*rá. The plural dative in á*n*rá is also of rare occurrence, the singular being more frequently used.

ání. This is the most usual plural suffix, being always used for the genitive and ablative; e. g.,

pa*kh*tání khund, the vale of poplars.

(7). The suffix e.

e is used in the sense of an indefinite article; e. g., *mard* 'man'; *marde* 'a man.'

The indefinite base formed by the suffix e is used as a base of inflection, the case endings following the e. Thus from *mardo* we get *mardeá* and *mardeár*.

ADJECTIVES.

1. Adjectives are formed by the terminations í, e*n*, ena, a*gh*, o, and e*gh* from nouns and adverbs; e. g.,

í.	demí, former	from	dem
	pha*dh*í, hinder	,,	pha*dh*á
e*n*, ena.	marde*n*, manly	,,	mard
	nu*gh*rae*n*, nu*gh*raena, } of silver	,,	nu*gh*ra
a*gh*.	ganda*gh*, bad	,,	gand
o.	gwá*th*o, windy	,,	gwá*th*
e*gh*.	dare*gh*, wooden	,,	dár

2. Adjectives precede nouns and generally take the termination e*n* when used with nouns, unless the original termination happens to be e*n*; as,

nu*gh*rae*n* áden, a silver mirror
but
gwá*th*oe*n* halwar, windy talk.

The adjectives jowai*n*, good, kisai*n*, small, and mazai*n*, great, form respectively before nouns jowáne*n*, kisáne*n*, and mazane*n*.

3. Comparison. The comparative degree is formed by the suffix thar, thir, or tar; e. g.,

kisai*n*	comp.	kisánthar and kasthar
burz	,,	burzáthir
mazai*n*	,,	masthar
jowai*n*	,,	jowánthar
sak	,,	sakthar,

the base being sometimes slightly modified. The word bathir (Pers. bihtar) is sometimes used with other adjectives to express comparison; as,

bathir ganda*gh*, worse.

The word geshtar "more" corresponds to the Pers. beshtar, but the positive is wanting in Balochí.

"Than" in comparison is expressed by azh, whether the adjective is put in the comparative degree or not; e. g.,

Azh tho ne*kh* e*n*, he is better than thou.

There is no special superlative form. The comparative form may be used, or the adverbs sakíá "extremely", hu*dh*áí "divinely" may be employed to give emphasis to the adjective. The phrase azh thewaghe*n* or azh kullá*n* "of all", may also be used with the comparative to give a superlative sense; e. g.,

Azh thewa*ghen* masthar, the greatest of all.

NUMERALS.

1. Cardinal Numbers.

Yak / Ya	One
Do	Two
Sai	Three
Chyár	Four
Phanch	Five
Shash	Six
Hapt	Seven
Hasht / Hazhd	Eight
Nuh	Nine
Dah	Ten
Yázhdah / Yázdah	Eleven
Dwázhdah / Dwázdah	Twelve
Se*n*zdah	Thirteen
Chyárdah	Fourteen
Phá*n*zdah	Fifteen
Shá*n*zdah	Sixteen
Havdah	Seventeen
Hazhdah	Eighteen
Nozd	Nineteen
Gíst	Twenty
Gíst-u-yak	Twenty-one
Gíst-u-do	Twenty-two, and so on regularly
Sí	Thirty
Chhil	Forty

Phanjáh	Fifty
Sai-gíst	Sixty
Saigíst-u-dah	Seventy
Chyár-gíst	Eighty
Chyárgíst-u-dah	Ninety
Sa*dh*	A hundred
Shazh-gíst	A hundred and twenty
Hapt-gíst	A hundred and forty
Hasht-gíst	A hundred and sixty
Nuh-gíst	A hundred and eighty
Dosa*dh*	Two hundred
Hazár } Ha*dh*ár }	A thousand
Lak	One hundred thousand
Khoṛ	An indefinitely large number.

The form *ya* "one" is used with nouns; ya is used by itself.

Counting from sixty upwards is usually done in multiples of twenty, intermediate numbers being reckoned on or back from the nearest multiple; e. g.,

217 is sai kham yázhdah-gíst, *i. e.*, three less eleven-twenties.

223 is yázhdah-gíst-o-sai, *i. e.*, eleven-twenties and three.

2. Ordinal Numbers.

Pheshí	First
Duhmí	Second
Saimí	Third
Chyárumí	Fourth
Phanchumí	Fifth
Shashumí	Sixth
Haptumí	Seventh
Hashtumí	Eighth
Nuhmí	Ninth
Dahmí	Tenth
Yázdamí	Eleventh
Dwázdamí	Twelfth
Se*n*zdamí	Thirteenth
Chyárdamí	Fourteenth
Phá*n*zdamí	Fifteenth
Shá*n*zdamí	Sixteenth
Havdamí	Seventeenth
Hazhdamí	Eighteenth

Nozdamí	Nineteenth
Gístumí	Twentieth
Síumí	Thirtieth
Chhilumí	Fortieth
Sa*dh*umí	Hundredth
Hazárumí	Thousandth

Compound numbers are treated as single words in forming the ordinal; as,

Gíst-yakumí	Twenty-first
Gíst-phanchumí	Twenty-fifth

3. Fractional Numbers.

one-half ($\frac{1}{2}$)	nem
one-third ($\frac{1}{3}$)	saiak
one-quarter ($\frac{1}{4}$)	páo, chyárak
one-fifth ($\frac{1}{5}$)	phanjak
three-quarters ($\frac{3}{4}$)	sai-páo
one and a half ($1\frac{1}{2}$)	yak nem or deḍh
with one half more	sáḍhoá*n*
e. g. four and a half ($4\frac{1}{2}$)	sáḍhoá*n* chyár

With minuter fractions the word bahr is employed with the ordinal number, as Gístumí bahr, one-twentieth.

4. Multiples.

a. Multiples of quantity, expressed in English by the word "fold."

dúrá	double
yake sai	threefold
yake chyár	fourfold
yake phanch	fivefold

and so on as required.

b. Multiples of time expressed generally by the word bar corresponding to the similar use of "times" in English. Bar is put in the plural except in ya-bare "once", where it receives the indefinite suffixes. Thí-bare "another time" is similarly constructed:

ya-bare	once
do-ḅará*n*	twice
sai-bará*n*	thrice
chyár-bará*n*	four times

and so on.

PRONOUNS.

I.—Personal Pronouns.

a. First person.

Singular.

Nom.	ma*n*, mah	I
Gen.	maní, maí*n*	my
	maí*gh*	mine
Dat. } Acc. }	maná*n*	me, to me
Instr. }	ma*n*	I, from me
Abl. }	azh ma*n*, go ma*n*	with me &c.

Plural.

Nom.	má	we
Gen.	maí*n*	our
	maí*gh*	ours
Dat. } Acc. }	már, márá	us, to us
Instr. } Abl. }	má	we, us, &c.

The plural má is often used with a singular signification.

b. Second person.

Singular.

Nom.	thau, tha	thou
Gen.	thaí	thy
	thaí*gh*	thine
Dat. } Acc. }	thará	thee, to thee
Instr. } Abl. }	thau, tha	thou, &c.

Plural.

Nom.	shawá, shá	you
Gen.	shawáí, sháí	your
	shawáí*gh*	yours
Dat. } Acc. }	shawár, shár	you
Instr. } Abl. }	shawá, shá &c.	you

The singular and plural in the second personal pronoun are generally confined to their proper significations.

II.—Third Personal Pronoun and Demonstrative Pronouns.

The demonstrative pronouns "this" and "that" take the place of the 3rd personal pronoun, which only exists independently in the form of the pronominal suffixes to be noticed hereafter.

1. Proximate demonstrative pronoun.

Singular.

Nom.	esh, e, í	this, he
Gen.	eshí, eshiyá	of this, his
Dat.	eshiyar	to this, to him
Acc.	eshiyá, eshiyar	this, him
Instr.	eshiyá	he
Abl.	'sh eshiyá, go eshiyá, &c.	from this, from him &c.

Plural.

Nom.	esh, eshá*n*	these, they
Gen.	eshání	of these, their
Dat.	eshá*n*rá	to these, to them
Acc.	eshá*n*, eshá*n*rá	these, them
Instr.	eshání	these, they
Abl.	'sh eshání &c.	from them &c.

An intensive form is used with the prefix ham, sometimes corrupted to haw, as hawe, hamesh, hameshiyá, hameshání &c., "this very one, by this one."

2. Remote demonstrative pronoun.

Singular.

Nom.	á*n*	that, he
Gen.	á*n*hí, á*n*hiyá	of that, his
Dat.	á*n*hiyar	to him, that
Acc.	á*n*hiyar, á*n*hiyá	that, him
Instr.	á*n*hiyá	that, he
Abl.	'sh á*n*hiyá &c.	from him &c.

Plural.

Nom.	á*n*há*n*, á*n*	those, they
Gen.	á*n*hání	of those, their.
Dat.	á*n*há*n*rá	to those, them
Acc.	á*n*há*n*, á*n*há*n*rá	those, them
Instr.	á*n*nání	those, they
Abl.	'sh á*n*hání &c.	from them &c.

This pronoun has also an intensive form with the prefix ham or haw, meaning "that one", "that very one", as hawá*n*, hawá*n*hiyá &c.

The compound forms imar and á*n*mar (for í-mard and á*n*-mard) are frequently used in the sense of personal pronouns and are applied even to animals and inanimate objects.

3. Pronominal suffixes.

These are frequently employed with the verb when the regular pronouns are not expressed. Those of the 3rd person, *í* "he" and *ish* "they" are most frequently employed, the distinction between the singular and plural forms not being carefully observed. (For examples, see under the verb.) The suffix á*n* is also sometimes used in the 3rd person as khu*th*a*gh*antá*n* "they did." The 1st person has also a suffix ú*n*, which is not so frequently used. With this suffix the verb takes a peculiar form, a euphonic t being inserted to strengthen the weak final nasal of the 1st person singular or plural, as khushtha*gh*á*n*tá*n* or khushtha*gh*ú*n*tú*n* "I or we killed."

III.—Relative Pronouns.

The word ki performs most of the duties of a relative pronoun, as in Persian, and often merely has the meaning of a relative particle, being indeclinable, so that the meaning is not complete without the use of other pronouns; e. g.,

E mard hameshe*n* ki eshiyá birá*th*á má giptha*gh*ú*n*, this is the man whose brother we have taken.

The following relative phrases are used :

har khas ki	whoever
har ki } har chí ki }	whatever
á*n* ki	who, whoever, whatever

e. g.,

har khas ki khá*kh*t, every one who comes
har ki thau gushe, whatever you say
a*n* ki khái' chí ká*dh*irá, whatsoever thing comes from God.

IV.—Reflectives.

Wa*th*, self.

Singular.

Nom.	wa*th*	self
Gen.	wa*th*í	own, one's own
Dat. } Acc. }	wa*th*ár	self

Plural.

Nom.	wa*th*á*n*	selves
Gen.	wa*th*ání	own
Dat. } Acc. }	wa*th*á*n*rá	selves

The words jind and but are also used in the sense of "self."

oneself, wa*th*í wa*th*
or wa*th*í jind

e. g.,

*Kn*mar wa*th*í jindár khushtha, he killed himself.

Jind is especially used in referring to one's own private property, as the Hindústání nij; e. g.,

hawe má*dh*in maní jinde*gh*en, this mare is my own property.

The phrase pha-wa*th*án is used for among themselves, ourselves, yourselves.

V.—Interrogatives.

Who, khái?

Sing. and Plur.

Nom.	khái	who?
Gen.	khái*gh*	whose?
Dat. Acc.	khájár	whom?

what?	chih
which, what (qualifying a noun)	ki*th*á*n* thá*n*
how much } how many? }	chi*kh*tar, chikar (P. chi qadr?)

VI.—Correlatives.

so much } so many }	ik*h*tar, ikar (P. ín qadr?)
just so much	hawi*kh*tar (P. hamín qadr?)
that much	á*n*khtar
just that much	hawá*n*khtar

VII.—Indefinite.

khase	any one, some one
har-khas	every one
khas ne*n*	nobody
hech } hechí } 'chí }	any
har-chí	everything
'chíe	something
'chíe-'chíe	a little
hechí-na } 'chí-na }	nothing

báz	many
kham	few
geshtar	more
kharde	some
yak-áptiyá	one another
thí / phi*th*í	other, another
thí khase	some one else
thí 'chie	something else
thí 'chí-na	nothing else
the*gh*í / thewa*ghen*	all
drust / kull / las	the whole
kullá*n*-phajyá	altogether
hardo	both

STRUCTURE OF THE VERB.

The simplest form or base of every verb is with one or two exceptions identical in form with the 2nd pers. sing. imperative. From this base are formed immediately, by the addition of certain terminations, the imperative, aorist, infinitive and present participle. The termination of the infinitive is a*gh*. From the base so obtained two more tenses, the present and imperfect, are formed. The past participle is formed from the base in a manner which will be described hereafter, and other past participles are formed from it as a base.

(*a*). Forms derived immediately from the base.

The imperative, as observed above, generally is the simplest form of the base. Verbs beginning with vowels take the prefix ba or bi, and the verbs wara*gh* "to eat" and rava*gh* "to go" also form their imperatives bawar and baro. Verbs beginning with vowels take also the prefix bi or kh in the aorist. These prefixes are not used either in the imperative or aorist when a negative is expressed, the negative particles na, ni and ma taking their place; e. g.,

riyár	bring
mayár	do not bring
bilá*n*	I will let
nelá*n*	I will not let
khái*th*	he will come
nayái*th*	he will not come

The prefix kh is most usually taken in the aorist, but the verb ila*gh* "to let" always takes b.

The aorist has both indefinite, present, future and subjunctive significations. The terminations are as follows :—

	Singular.	Plural.
1.	*án*	ú*n*, om
2.	e	e*th*, e*dh*, ̄e
3.	th, *th*, í*th*, í	ant

The most usual termination of the 3rd person singular is í*th*, which often becomes simply í. The following take th :—

Infinitive	3rd pers. sing. aorist.
khana*gh*, to do	khanth
jana*gh*, to strike	janth or jath
gira*gh*, to take	gírth
bara*gh*, to take away	bárth
wara*gh*, to eat	wárth

In gira*gh*, gír is the radical form of the verb. In bara*gh* and wara*gh* the radical vowel is lengthened. The following take *th* ;—

bía*gh* to be	bí*th*, bí
rava*gh* to go	ro*th*, ro
dea*gh* to give	dá*th*, dá
sía*gh* to swell	sí*th*

The present participle used of a continued or repeated action is formed from the base by the termination ána ; e. g.,

Infinitive	Present Participle.
bía*gh*	bíána
khana*gh*	khanána

The infinitive in a*gh* is a noun and can be inflected. The inflected form has a gerundial signification ; e. g.,

khana*gh*, to do, doing.

khana*gh*á khapta-í, he began to do (lit. he fell a-doing).

The present and imperfect are formed from the infinitive by the following terminations :

PRESENT.

	Sing.	Plur.
1.	án	áú*n*, áom
2.	e	e, e*th*
3.	e*n*	ant, an, e*n*

IMPERFECT.

1.	a*th*án	a*th*ú*n*
2.	a*th*e	a*th*e
3.	a*th*, e*th*	a*th*ant

The past participle is formed by the addition of the suffix tha or *tha* to the base which is liable to modifications to be noted below. For purposes of composition the past base ends in *gh*. (See sounds, *gh*.) From the base so formed the perfect and pluperfect are formed by the following terminations:

PERFECT.

1.	*án*	ú*n*, om
2.	e	e, e*th*
3.	—	ant

PLUPERFECT.

1.	a*thán*	a*thún*
2.	a*the*	a*the*
3.	a*th*, á	a*th*ant

The 3rd pers. singular of the perfect is the simple form of the past participle without the *gh*. In transitive verbs with an object and agent, this form expresses the perfect throughout, the agent being in the inflected or instrumental form, while the object is uninflected; *e. g.*,

mardumá na*gh*an wártha, the man ate bread,

where mardumá is the inflected form of mardum. But—

mardum na*gh*anár wárth, the man will eat bread.

Here mardum is uninflected and naghan receives the objective inflection.

The terminations of the present are nearly identical with those of the perfect, and those of the imperfect, with the pluperfect. Both seem to be formed by the addition of the present and past forms of the defective verb *to be* to the infinitive base and the past base respectively. The present with the infinitive base forms the present, with the past base the perfect. Similarly the past forms the imperfect and pluperfect. These forms are as follows:

PRESENT.

Sing.		Plur.	
I am	*án*	we are	ú*n*
thou art	e	you are	e
he is	e*n*	they are	ant

PAST.

I was	a*thán*	we were	a*thún*
thou wast	a*the*	you were	a*the*
he was	a*th*	they were	a*th*ant

The plural forms ú*n*, e, a*thún*, a*the*, when used with a pronoun immediately preceding, take the prefix kh; *e. g.*,

má khú*n*	we are
má kha*thún*	we were

But this prefix is never used when a noun or adjective immediately precedes.

From the simple past participle which has both an active and passive signification are formed two other participles; *viz.*, (1) the active past participle, used of a completed action and only found before a verb in a past tense. This is formed by changing the termination tha, *tha* into tho. (2) The present participle used of a continued but not repeated action. This is formed by changing tha or *tha* in thíyá, *th*íyá or sometimes thí*gh*á, *thígh*á.

The use of the four participles may be shown as follows:

Past	dára*gh*, to hold. dáshtha, held. dáshto, having held.
Present	dáshthíyá or dáshthí*gh*á, holding, continuing to hold. dárána, holding (with intervals), keeping on taking hold.

Formation of the Past Participle.

The termination is either *th*a or tha which is added to the base. *Tha* is the more usual. It is taken by all verbs whose bases end in a vowel. Verbs ending in mutes take *th*a as a rule, with a short vowel inserted after the characteristic; *e. g.*, bashka*gh* "to give," P. P. bashka*tha*. When a verb corresponds with a Persian verb in ídan, a short i is sometimes inserted; *e. g.*,

rasa*gh*, to arrive P. P. rasi*th*a (P. rasídan).
thursa*gh*, to fear P. P. thursi*th*a (P. tursídan).

When tha is used it is always attached to the base without an intervening vowel. This leads frequently to the modification of the characteristic of the base, the changes corresponding closely with those which take place in Persian. In some verbs the vowel of the base is also changed, and others are wholly irregular. Verbs whose characteristic is n (a class which includes all causals) take the termination tha without any modification of the base.

The most usual changes of characteristic letters are sh and zh to *kh*, f to p, *dh* and z to s. Many verbs in sh and s, take the termination without modifying the characteristic.

The following list gives the past participles of all the irregular verbs, also most of those which form their past participle by taking tha without modification of the base. The verbs beginning with vowels which take the prefixes b, bi and kh in the imperative and aorist are also given.

Infinitive		Past Participle
ára*gh*	to bring	ártha
ása*gh*	to rise	ástha
ashkhana*gh*	to hear	ashkhu*th*a
á*gh*	to come	á*kh*tha, átka

Infinitive.		Past Participle.
aksa*gh*	to sleep	akastha
ila*gh*	to let	ishtha
oshta*gh*	to stand	oshtá*th*a
oshtalaina*gh* (causal of oshtagh)		oshtalaintha.
(The above take the prefixes b, bi, and kh.)		
bása*gh*	to low	bástha
bá*gh*	to be killed	bái*th*a
bara*gh*	to take away	burtha
bresa*gh*	to spin	brestha
bushka*gh*	to discharge (a gun)	bu*kh*tha
bozha*gh*	to open	bo*kh*tha
banda*gh*	to shut, tie	bastha
bía*gh*	to be	bí*th*a
phadea*gh*	to run	phadá*th*a
phrusha*gh*	to burst	phrushtha
phasha*gh*	to cook	phakká
thusa*gh*	to faint	thustha
thosa*gh*	to extinguish	thostha
thasha*gh*	to run, gallop	tha*kh*tha
thásha*gh*	to gallop (a horse)	thá*kh*tha
já*gh*	to chew	jái*th*a
jana*gh*	to strike	ja*th*a
china*gh*	to pick up	chi*th*a
dina*gh*	to tear	dirtha
dosha*gh*	to milk	dushtha
dosha*gh*	to sew	do*kh*tha
do*gh*	to fetch water	do*th*a
dea*gh*'	to give	dá*th*a
rava*gh*	to go	shu*th*a, shu*dh*a, raptha
ru*dh*a*gh*	to grow	rustha
ra*dh*a*gh*	to tear up	rastha
runa*gh*	to reap	rutha, runtha
resina*gh*	to pursue	resintha
rísha*gh*	to scatter, pour	ri*kh*tha
zá*gh*	to bring forth	zá*th*a
zána*gh*	to know	zántha
zina*gh*	to snatch	zítha, zi*th*a
zíra*gh*	to raise	zurtha
susha*gh*	to burn, be burnt	su*kh*tha
sosha*gh*	to burn (tr.)	so*kh*tha
sinda*gh*	to break	sistha

Infinitive.		Past Participle.
sía*gh*	to swell	sí*tha*
shu*dhagh*	to hunger	shustha
sho*dhagh*	to wash	shustha
shasta*gh*	to send	shastá*tha*
shamúsha*gh*	to forget	shamushtha
shawashka*gh*	to sell	shawa*kh*tha
khasha*gh*	to pull, turn out	khashtha
khisha*gh*	to cultivate	khishtha
khusha*gh*	to kill	khushtha
khafa*gh*	to fall	khaptha
khana*gh*	to do	khu*tha*
kiza*gh*	to allow	kishtha
gá*gh*	to copulate	gá*tha*
grá*dhagh*	to boil	grástha
garda*gh*	to return	gartha
gira*gh*	to take	giptha
gire*gh*	to weep	girentha
guza*gh*	to pass	gwastha
gusha*gh*	to speak	gwashtha
galá*gh*	to praise	galái*tha*
ginda*gh*	to see	dí*tha*
gwáfa*gh*	to summon	gwáptha
gwara*gh*	to rain	gwartha
gwafa*gh*	to weave	gwaptha
gezha*gh*	• to bear abortion	gi*kh*tha
gíesha*gh*	to pay, pick out	gíeshtha
láina*gh*	to touch	lai*tha*
la*gh*usha*gh*	to slip	la*gh*ushtha
lawásha*gh*	to drink	lawáshtha
ma*dhagh*	to freeze	mastha
mira*gh*	to die	murtha
mi*rag*h	to fight	mi*ratha*
mizha*gh* meza*g*h	} to urine	mishtha
misha*gh*	to suck	mishtha
musha*gh*	to rub	mushtha
nigosha*gh*	to listen	nigoshtha
ninda*gh*	to sit	nishtha
nyá*dhagh*	to post	nyástha
wána*gh*	to read	wántha
wapsa*gh*	to sleep	waptha

Infinitive.		Past Participle.
wara*gh*	to eat	wártha
husha*gh*	to dry	hushtha

Causals. The causal is commonly formed by adding the suffix ain to the root; e. g.,

tharagh, to return.
tharainagh, to cause to return, *i. e.*, to give back.

Oshta*gh* "to stand," and ninda*gh* "to sit," form their causals thus:—

oshta*gh*—oshtalaina*gh*.
ninda*gh*—nishtaina*gh* (to lay, spread out.)

Some of the verbs given in the above list are causals, the intransitive verb becoming transitive by a change in the radical vowel resembling the Sanskrit guṇa or vṛiddhi, see—

susha*gh*, sosha*gh*; thasha*gh*, thásha*gh*; thusa*gh*, thosa*gh*.

Compound Verbs. Verbs are compounded with prepositions, with nouns and with other verbs. The most common of those compounded with prepositions will be found under the words ایر er "down," مان mán "in;" در dar "out;" and گون gon "with" in the vocabulary. In verbs which take the prefixes bi, b, and kh these are inserted after the prepositions, as are also the negative particles na and ma; e. g.,

phajyá together. Ara*gh* to bring.
phajyá ára*gh*, to recognize.
phajyá khárí*th*, he will recognize.
phajyá nayártha, he did not recognize.

Compound phrases of a noun and a verb are common. The verb, khana*gh* "to do," dea*gh* "to give," jana*gh* "to strike," and gira*gh* "to take" are most commonly used in this way; e. g.,

sar gira*gh*, to set out
dem dea*gh*, to send

One verb frequently qualifies another, the two verbs being used in the same tense and person throughout. The active past participle is never used unless followed by another past tense; e. g.,

ila*gh* dea*gh*, to let go
bilá*n* deá*n*, I will let go
ishtho dá*th*a, he let go
thara*gh* á*gh*, to come back
thará*n* khá*n*, I will come back
thar*th*o á*kh*tha*gh*a*th*á*n*, I had come back

The particles i and ish. These particles are appended to verbs and take the place of the pronouns of the 3rd person when not expressed before the verb. The singular form is í and the plural ish, but in practice they are used almost indiscriminately. They express (1) the agent of the verb in the 3rd person; (2) the object of an action, or the instrument by which it was performed; e. g.,

(1) khu*th*a, did or done
án khu*th*a or khu*th*a-í, } he did
ravag*h*a*th*ant-í, they were going
ja*th*a-ish, they struck
hechí nesta*th*-í, there was none of it (lit. anything it was not).

(2) wa*th* gindí*th*-í, he will see himself
ma*n* kharán-í, I will bring it
harkhas phajyá-khárí*th*-í, every one recognizes him.

Verbal Noun. From most verbs a verbal noun of agency can be formed by the suffix o*kh* being added to the base; e. g.,

gira*gh*, to take; giro*kh*, taker, creditor
khusha*gh*, to kill; khusho*kh*, murderer.

ADVERBS.

A great part of the Balochí adverbs are more properly adverbial phrases, only a few being original adverbs. Many are nouns in oblique cases, others phrases of several words.

(1.)—Adverbs of Time.

now	ní, ní*n*
then	ha*dhen*, *án*-va*kh*tá
when?	kha*dhen*
to-day	maroshí, mar'shí
yesterday	zí
the day before yesterday	phairí
three days ago	phisphairí
last night	doshí
night before last	pharandoshí
to-morrow	bánghá, bánghavá
the day after to-morrow	thí bánghá, phi*th*í-roshe
in the evening	begahá

to-morrow evening	bánghá-begahá, nawáshí-begahá
now-a-days	nínava*kh*tá, maroshí-nawáshí
formerly	olá
first, before	pheshá
afterwards	pha*dh*á
hitherto	she*dh*-pheshá
henceforward	she*dh*-pha*dh*á, she*dh*-demá
yet, till now, hitherto	dái*n*, dání, dánkoh, daníkará
always, perpetually	harro
now and then at one time and another	damdame, dame dame
once	yabare
at once	yabará
again	a*gh*, a*gh*dí, a*gh*a*th*á*n*
then, again	guḍá
another time	thíbare
at last	áhirá
early	phage*n*
at daybreak	rosh-tiká

(2).—Adverbs of Place.

a. Rest in a place.

here	e*dh*, e*dh*á, hame*dh*, hame*dh*á
there	o*dh*, ọ*dh*á, hamo*dh*, hamo*dh*á
before, in front of	demá
behind	pha*dh*á, dímá, pha-dímá
near	nazí, nazí*kh*
far	dír
out	dar
outside	darrá
above	khar*gh*á, burzá
below	jahlá, sher, buná
down	er
on, ahead	sará
where ?	bakhú ?
on this side	i*n*bará, shi*n*bará
beyond, on that side	á*n*bará, shá*n*bará
everywhere	harhandá
nowhere	thíhandá
elsewhere	hizhgarne*n*
anywhere	hizhgar.
in the middle	nyámá

b. Direction to or from.

hither	phe*dh*, phe*dhá*, i*n*go, i*n*gwar
thither	pho*dh*, pho*dhá*, á*n*go, á*n*gwar, phawá*n*go
hence	she*dh*, she*dhá*, shame*dhá*, shi*n*go
thence	sho*dh*, sho*dhá*, shamo*dhá*, shá*n*go
whither ?	thá*n*go ?
whence ?	ashkho ?
in this direction	i*n*-phalawá
in that direction	a*n*-phalawá
from this direction	'shí*n* phalawá
from that direction	'shá*n*-phalawá
in every direction	har-phalawá
in what direction ?	thá*n*-phalawá ?
onwards, upwards	sará
downwards	erá, sherí -pahná*dhá*
from above downwards	sará-erá
inwards	andará
outwards	darrá

(3).—Adverbs of Quantity.

much, many	báz
few, little, less	kham
a little	chíklo
very little	khamro
more	geshtar
enough	gwas, bas
a great deal, any amount	khoṛ

(4).—Adverbs of Manner, &c.

From most adjectives an adverb of quality or manner may be formed by the suffix *iyá*, the adjective being sometimes slightly modified ; e. g.,

ganda*gh*, bad	ganda*gh*iyá, badly
jowai*n*, good	jowániyá, well

Other adverbs of manner are :

very	sakíá, sakí*ghá*
together	phajíá
quickly	*zíṭhen*

perhaps	nawá*n*, kaïzá*n*
why?	pharche
altogether, certainly, doubtless	mundo, be-shak
thus	hanchho, hachho
how?	chachho? cho*n*?
in this way	e-ranga, e-r'gá
in that way	á*n*rangá, ár'gá
every way	harrangá
in what way?	thá*n*rangá
never	hechí-na, 'chína, mundo na

PREPOSITIONS.

There are few prepositions, properly speaking, in Balochí, as most of the particles so used follow the noun and would be more correctly called postpositions.

The following are prepositions proper and precede the noun which is governed in the oblique form (ablative or locative).

go	with, together with, in company with
gwar	with, near, in possession of
pha	on, for, among
ma*n*, má*n*	in, into
da*n*	into, to, up to
azh, ash, shi	from, than
avr	on, into

From the above, some prepositional phrases are formed, of which the first member precedes, and the last follows the governed noun.

go—gon	in company with
go—phajyá	together
azh—siwá	except
azh—darrá	without
pha—randá	on the track of
azh—phalawá	away, from
azh—pha*dh*á	behind

The postpositions do not put the noun governed in an oblique tense in the singular. The force is often that of the genitive, which has no distinct form in the singular, but as might be expected the genitive plural is often used. Pronouns also take the genitive in the singular.

on	sará
on, upon	chakhá
towards	nem*gh*á, ne*gh*á, phalawá
on account of	sángá
along with	phajya
in	nyámá, nyá*n*wá*n*
out of	darrá
near	khund, gwará
before, in front of	demá
behind, after	pha*dh*á
before (in time)	pheshá
over	sará, khar*gh*á
under	buná
beyond	'shá*n*bará
on this side of	'shi*n*bara
for, on account of	phar
in the presence of	rúbarú
in, in the middle of	láfá
like	ḍaulá, wájh

Examples.

khoh buná	under the hill
khoháni sará	on the hills
go wa*th*í sardárá	with his own chief
dro*gh* pha ímáná khátáe*n*	falsehood is a blot upon honour
dast jant avr barziyá	she puts her hand into the bag
eshiyá pha*dh*á	after this
thaí sángá	on your account
bozhí láfá	in the boat

CONJUNCTIONS.

also, too	dí
both, and	dí, dí
and, then	guḍá
and (copulative between nouns)	o
when	va*kh*tá-ki
whenever	á*n*-va*kh*tá-ki, har-va*kh*tá-ki, har-velá-ki
wherever	har-handá-ki, handá-ki

whithersoever	har-phalawá-ki
if	ki
that	ki
but	lekin (rare)
or	ki, hai
either, or	hai, hai
neither, nor	na, na
not	na
„ (with imperatives)	ma
else, otherwise	na
lest	cho-ma-ví-ki
because, in order that	hawe-sangá-ki
although	a*gh*archi (rare)
until	dái*n* ki
as, like as	cho*n*-ki, chachho*n*-ki

INTERJECTIONS.

yes	hau !
yes, certainly	bale !
no	na, inná
see there	gind
behold	marvehí
yes, sir	wázhá !
my lord	wázhá maní, sái*n* !
welceme !	biyá durr sh'á*kh*te, biyá*th*ai
all's well	mahairá
well done	wáh
bismi'lláh	in God's name
salám alaik, alaik salám	greetings between Musalmáns
phrr	fie !
O	halloa.

LIST OF ABBREVIATIONS.

A. Ar.	...	Arabic.	Poet.	...	Poetical.
P.	...	Persian.	Adj.	...	Adjective.
Panj.	...	Panjabí.	Adv.	...	Adverb.
P.P.	...	Past Participle.	Prep.	...	Preposition.
S.	...	Substantive.	Br.	...	Brahoi.
Si.	...	Sindhí	M.	...	Masculine.
Skr.	...	Sanskrit.	F.	...	Feminine.
V.	...	Verb.	Cf.	...	Compare.
			H.	...	Hindí.

Note.—The Arabic letters ق ع ظ ط ض ص ح are not used in this vocabulary, having no distinct pronunciation. They are represented by ک ت ز س ه and ا when they occur in borrowed words.

VOCABULARY.

آ ا

(Words beginning with vowels.)

آب Ab, P. (metaphorically) honour, dignity. Not used in the meaning water. (Ab er-kana*gh*) to disgrace.

ابا Abbá, A. Br. father, papa. (Used by children.)

آبا Ubbá, Si. north.

ابتر Abtar, hyæna, (P. kaftár.)

آبریشم Abresham, P. silk.

ابناخ Abná*kh*, P. honourable, worthy.

آبہار Ubhár, Si. raising. (Poet. in the phrase 'uchál-ubhár' lowering and raising.)

آپتیا Aptiyá. Only in the phrase 'yak áptiyá,' among themselves.

اپورس Apúrs, (P. ávran, árus) the Juniper tree. (*Juniperus excelsa.*)

اپہان Aphán, a leather bag for flour.

آپہرغ Aphira*gh*, p.p. áphirta, (Si. áphirjṇu) to swell.

اث A*th*, was. 3rd pers. singular of past indef. of the verb to be. The complete tense is a*th*án, a*th*eí, a*th*, a*th*ún, a*th*eí, a*th*ant or a*th*an.

آچال Uchál. S. See Ubhár.

اچا Achá, (Si. achho) clean.

آجام Ajám, (P. anjám) settlement, arrangement.

اجب Ajab, (A. عجب) wonderful. Ajab-rang, beautiful, purple-coloured.

آخرا A*kh*irá, A. utterly, extremely.

ادب Adab, A. good manners.

آدت Ádit,
آدتوار Áditwár, } Si. Panj, Sunday.

ادغ Ada*gh*, v., to pitch a tent, encamp.

آدین Áden,
ازینه Ázína, } a mirror.

اڈ Aḍ, Si. a masonry watercourse.

اڈ دیئغ Aḍ-dea*gh*, v., to lean.

اڈا Aḍḍá, Si. Br. brother (familiarly).

آڈرغ Uḍra*gh*, (Si uḍirṇu,) to fly.

آڈوهي Uḍohí, Si. a white ant.

اڈي Aḍḍí, S. Br. sister (familiarly).

آرام Áram, P. rest.

آرتهه Árth (P. árad) flour.

آرد Urd, an army. (P. urdú.)

ارزان Arzán, adj. P. cheap.

ارسي Ársí, adj. Si. idle.

آرغ Ára*gh*, p.p. ártha; imp. bi-ár; fut. khárá*n*. (P. ávardan, bi-ár) to bring. Kárá ára*gh*, to use. Phajyá ára*gh*, to recognize. Gír-ára*gh*, to remember.

ارمان Armán, pity. P.

آروخ Áro*kh*, bringer. Verbal noun from ára*gh*.

آریغ Arí*kh*, gums.

ازاب دئیغ Azáb-dea*gh*, A. Bi. to offend.

آزاد Azád, free. P.

اِزبوخت Izbo*kh*t, the ajwain seed.

ازمان Azmán,
اژمان Azhmán, } the sky. (P. ásmán.)

آزماینغ Ázmáina*gh*, to examine. P.

آزموتا Ázmútá, examination.

اژ Azh, from. (P. az. Pázand ezh.)

اژگژ Azhgizh, flint and steel. (Cf. P. az*kh*ash.)

اژمان Azhmán. See Azmán.

اژورک izhwark,
اژرک izhrak,
اژگ izhg,
} (Br. shark.) *Rhazya stricta.*

آس ás, fire. (P. átish).

آس روخ ás-ro*kh*, a platform erected where funeral ceremonies have been performed.

آس کهوه ás-khoh, flint (lit. firestone).

آسان ásán, easy. P.

اسپ asp, horse. (The generic term.) P.

آسپست uspust, lucerne grass.

اسپهلک isphulk, the spleen. Br.

استا astá,
استث astath,
} was.

استین aste*n*,
استنت astant,
} is, are.

} Parts of the defective verb to be, to exist. (P. hastan. Sk. As.)

استار astár, star. (P. sitára.)

استرغ istara*g*h, razor.

آستغ ástagh, slowly. (P. áhista.)

استور istúr, coarse, thick.

آستین ástín, sleeve. P.

استین istín, a light cloud, cirrhus.

اسر asr (a. اثر), impression.

اسر asur, dawn, morning twilight. Si.

آسر ásur (a. آصر), mercy.

اسرار isrár, mystery, secret. A.

آسروخ ásro*kh*, the third day of mourning. A platform erected to commemorate it.

آسغ ása*gh*, p.p. ástha, fut. khásá*n*, imp. biás, to rise. *Ásán*, rising. Rosh-ásán, sunrise.

آسک ásk, a deer (f.) (P. áhú.)

آسک مهسک ásk-mahisk, a kind of fly.

اسل asul (a. اصل), original.

اسلا asulá, from the first. Asulá ganno*kh*, a born idiot.

آسن ásin, iron. (Cf. P. áhan.)

اشا asbá, a. eight o'clock in the evening.

اش ash, from. (P. az.)

اش کوه ash-koh, whence?

اش موذا ash-mod*h*á (for azh hamo*dh*á), thence.

اش میذا ashme*dh*á (for azh hame*dh*á), hence.

اشتافي ashtáfí, s. quickness. (P. shitábí.)

اشکنغ ashkana*gh*, p.p. ashku*th*a, imp. bi ashkun, to hear, listen. Compounded of ash-knana*gh*. (Ash = Skr. asru.)

اِشتهر ishtha, p.p. of ilagh. q. v.

اُشتغ ushta*gh*. See اوشتغ oshta*gh*.

اغ a*gh*, adv. conj. again, then.

آغ á*gh*, p.p. á*kh*tha, imp. biyá, fut. khá*n*, (P. ámadan, biyá), to come.

phe*dh* á*gh*e*n*, mana-á*gh*e*n*, } is coming.
er-á*gh*, to come down.
dar-á*gh*, come out.
mán-á*gh*, be applied, suit, hit.
Phá*dh*-á*gh*, rise.
dast-á*gh*, get, come to hand.
kárá-á*gh*, be of use.

آغاهي á*gh*ábí, warning. (P. ágáh.)

اغدي a*gh*dí, again. Also اغ a*gh*. q. v.

اغر a*gh*ar, if. (P. agar.)

اعرچه a*gh*archi, although (rare).

اغل a*gh*l (a. عقل), intellect.

اغما a*gh*má, effort, endeavour.

آف áf, water. (P. áb, Z. áfs.)

آف آروخ áf-áro*kh*, آفي áfí, } water-bearer.

آف بيئغ áf-bía*gh*, to melt, thaw.

آف داري áf dárí, irrigation.

آف ديئغ áf-dea*gh*, to irrigate.

آف شیف áf-shef, slope, watershed.

آف لغر áf-laghar, rapid, waterfall.

آف مُرغ áf-murgh, waterfowl.

آف درك áf-drik, a kind of grass. (Panj. manihár.)

آفسن áfsin, pregnant. (Cf. P. ábista.)

آفشک áfshik, s. soup. (Cf. P. áb-zah.)

آفکن áfkin, box for holding collyrium.

افیم áfím, opium. (A. afyún.)

إکتر iktar,
اکر ikar, } so much, thus much. (? P. I'n ḳadr.)

اکس akas, envy.

اکسغ aksagh, p.p. akastha, fut. kaksí, imp. biakas, to sleep.

اکسرا aksará, generally.

اکل akul (a. عقل), intellect, wits.

آکهان ákhán, proverb, anecdote. Si.

آکهر ákhar, buttermilk. Si.

آکهیرو ákhero, nest. Si.

آکیا ukaiyá, in that way, of that sort.

الیلا akíla (a. عقیله), celebrated.

اگ ag, rate of sale..

الاج iláj, cure. (A. علاج)

الاهده aláhida, separate. (A. علیحده)

آلسي álsí, idle. Si.

إلغ ilagh, p.p. ishtha, fut. kilf. imp. bil. (P. hishtan, hil), to leave, abandon. ilagh-deagh, p.p. ishtho-dátha, to let go.

الکه ulkah, the world, the universe.

امب amb, mango. P.

امبازي ambází, embrace. (P. ham, bázú.)

امبر ambur, forceps. P.

امبراه ambráh, servant, companion. (? P. hamráh.)

امبل ambal, mistress, lover; companion.

آمدن ámdan, income. (P. ámdan, to come.)

امرا imar, he, this man, this. For in mard.

آمر umar, age. (Ar. عمر).

امّر ámur, slowly.

امسرو amsaro, equal in age or otherwise.

امل amul, mistress (see ambal).

امسوف amso*dh*, grief. (Cf. P. afsos).

امنام annám, namesake. (P. hamnám.)

امیر amír, chief.

آن a*n*, dem. pro. that, he.

آنهي a*n*hí. } Genitive of *án*.
آنهیا a*n*hiyá. }

آنهیار a*n*hiyár. Objective and dative of *án*.

آنبر anbar, } beyond, on that side.
آنبرا anbará, }

اِدابر inbará, on this side.

انجیر anjír, s. fig ; khohí anjír, wild fig. P. see *hinjir*.

اندرا andará, adv. inside.

آندیما ándemá, adv. thither, that side.

اِندیما indemá, adv. hither, this side.

انساف insáf, s. justice. (A. انصاف.)

انزي a*n*zí, s. a tear. P.

آنکتر á*n*ktar, } so much, as much as that. (?. P. ánqadr.)
آنکر á*n*kar, }

انگارا á*n*gárá, Tuesday. Si.

انگني anga*ne*, innumerable. Si.

آنگو á*n*go, thither, in that direction.

انگو i*n*go, hither, in this direction.

انماچه anmácha, an ammunition pouch. See *hambácha*.

آنمر á*n*mar, he, that man, that. (For á*n* mard.)

آنو ánú, egg. Si.

انهالا unhálá, hot weather. Si.

انیشغ aníshag*h*, s. (P. anúsha), forehead ; fate, fortune.

آوار áwár, spoil, plunder.

آوار áwár, mixed. P. *Áwár bíagh*, to mix with, join.

آواز áwáz, voice. P.

اوباسي obásí, yawn.

اوبهر obhar, east. Si.

اوتک otak, s. a halt; otak khana*gh*, to halt, encamp.

اوتهر othar, s. a dust-storm.

اوٹغ oṭi*gh*, s. } a tank.
اوٹي oṭí, s. }

اوجاغو ojá*gh*o, awake. Si.

اوجري ojrí, stomach. Si. Paj. See sa*ghin*dán.

آوداري ávdárí, s. irrigation.

اور avr, on, upon, into. (Pázand, awar, on, over.)

اوڈا o*dh*á, adv. there.

اوزار auzár, tool.

اوزي iwazí, revenge, substitute. (A. عوضي.)

اورزا awarzá, pleasing, agreeable.

اوشتغ oshta*gh*, v. p.p. oshtá*th*a: imp. bosht, to stand, stay. (P. istádan.)

اوشتلينغ oshtalaina*gh*. Causal of *oshtag*h, to post, set up.

اوگال ogál, chewing the cud. (Si. Ogár.)

اولا olá, adv. formerly. (From A. اول.)

اولک olak, beasts of burden. (? Turkish wulá*gh*.)

اولهه olah, west. Si.

اولي olí, adj. former.

اوندو ondo, overturned. Si. Ondo khana*gh*, to upset.

آوهسان کهتا auhsán-khatá, a puzzle.

اوهي obí, } flame.
اوهيل ohíl, }

اوير aver, late. Si.

آه áh, in, ah! alas!

اهار ahár, the hot weather, the month Ásárḥ (Si. Panj. Ahar).

اهسان ahsán, mankind. (A. aḥsán.)

آهنجغ áhanja*gh*, a sash, kamarband. P.

اي e or í, prep, this.

ايرگا er'gá, } in this way.
ايرنگا erangá, }

ايذ e*dh*, } adv. here. (Cf. Zend. aétadha.)
ايذا e*dh*á, }

اير er, adv. down, below. شير sh'er, from below. (Cf. P. zer, below.)

ايرغ er-á*gh*, to come down.

ايربرغ er-bara*gh*, to swallow.

ايرجذغ er-jana*gh*, to cast down, abase.

ايرشفغ er-shafa*gh*, to go down, set (of the sun). p.p. er-shu*th*a.

ايروغ er-rava*gh*, to go down.

ايرشف er-shaf, s. going down. Rosh-er-shaf, sunset.

ايركهفغ er-khafa*gh*, v. to descend, alight.

ايركهذغ er-khana*gh*, v. to lay down, place.

ايرگوات er-gwá*th*, the lee-side; er-gwá*th*á, to lee-ward.

ايرنذدغ er-ninda*gh*, v. to sit down.

ايش esh, this. (Cf. Zend. aesha.)

ياهان ímán, honour.

اين ín, pron. this.

ايو aiv, spot, bolt. (A. عيب.)

ايوكها ewakhá, alone. (Panj. hekwá.)

ب B.

بادشاه bádsháh, king. P.

بار bár, s. burden, load. P.
bár-banda*gh*, to load.
bár-er-khana*gh*, to unload.

بارغ bára*gh*, adj. fine, thin, lean. (P. báŕík.)

بارو báro, } turn. Si.
بارے báre, }

بارتهه báṛth, 3rd pers. sing. fut. of bara*gh*.

باز báz, many, much.
bázen wájhá, of many sorts.
bazen barán, often.
bázen rangá, many coloured.

بازار bázár, bazaar. P.

بازو bázú, limb. P.

بازيگر bázígar, juggler.

باسغ básagh, v. to low (of cattle).

باغ bágh, s. a garden. P.

باغ bágh, v. p.p. báitha بائٹه, to be killed.

باغار bágh*ár, s. a lizard.

باقي báqí, adj. remaining. A.

بال bál, s. flight.
bál-giragh, to fly, take flight.
bál-deagh, to let fly.

بالاذ báládh, figure, shape, form.

بالاذيا báládhiyá, adv. from below, upwards.

بالغ bálagh, of age. A.

باندي bándí, s. a hostage.

بانگ báng, a voice, sound; cock-crow. P.

بانگا bángá, } s. the morning. Bángawá, in the morning
بانگو bángo, } to-morrow. Thí-bánga, the day after to-morrow.

بانگوهنا bángohiná, in the early morning.

باندن bándan, a rough table.

باؤت báut, refugee.

باؤتي báutí, shelter, refuge.

باهر bábir, s. a herd of donkeys.

باهرو báhrav, s. male calves.

بپها baphá, scurf. Si. bapho.

بت but, self, oneself. (Si. butu, the body).

بتار bitár, the two stars (forming the tail of *Ursa major*).

بتهر bathir, better, very good. (P. bihtar.)

بتهلو bathlo, wooden mortar.

بٹيره baterá, quail. Si.

بج bij, seed. Panj.

بچهه bachh, son. P.

بخت ba*kh*t, fortune. P.

بخت والا ba*kh*twálá, fortunate, generous, (used in addressing superiors).

بختہ bu*kh*ta, p.p. of bushka*gh*. q. v.

بخمل ba*kh*mal, velvet. (P. ma*kh*mal.)

بد bad, bad (only in Persian compounds).

بدخو bad-khú, ill-natured.

بددوا bad-duá, curse.

بدشکل bad-shakl, ugly,

بدرگا badragá, an escort.

بدي badí, enmity. P.

بڈغ buḍa*gh*, v. p.p. بڈٹھ buḍa*th*a, to drown, be flooded. (Si. buḍaṇu.)

بذ ba*dh*, s. enemy. Generally in the plural بذان ba*dhán*.

بذل ba*dh*al, s. a debt.

بر bar, a time, a season. P.
ya-bare, once.
thí-bare, again. Báz*en*-bará*n*, often.

بر bar, s. fruit.

بر bar, s. a desert. A.

براث birá*th*, s. brother. Birá maní, my brother!

براخ bará*kh*, coarse grass found in the lower Sulaiman Hills.

براذر bará*dh*ar, s. brother (poet). P.

براذري bará*dh*arí, s. brotherhood.

برازاخت birázá*kh*t, s. a nephew, (brother's son). P. birádarzáda.

براور baráwar, adj. equal.

بردست bardast, s. shoulder-blade (used in augury).

برز burz,
برزا burzá,
برزغ burza*gh*, } adj. high. upper, lofty. P.

برزاتهر burzáthir, adj. very lofty, higher or highest. Comp. of burz.

برزي barzí, s. a bag.

برغ bara*gh*, v. p.p. buṛtha بڑتهه, to carry away, bear off, remove.
P. burdan.
Er-bara*gh*, to swallow.
Dar-bera*gh*, to defend, save.

برغ bura*gh*, v. p.p. buri*th*a برته, to cut. *P. burídan.*

برقه burqa, s. a veil. A.

برنج birinj, s. husked rice. P.

برو baro,
بروىث baroe*th*, } 2nd pers. sing. and plural Imperative of ravagh, go, go ye. P. burú. Skr. bhrú.

بروتهه baroth, s. moustaches. (Cf. Pashto bret.)

بريسغ bresag*h*, v. pp. brestha بريستهه, to spin.

بزي buzí, s. a spring.

بز baz, adj. thick, coarse.

بز buz, s. a goat. P.

بشام bashám, the rains, the month of Sáwan.

بشک bushk, s. a horse's mane.

بشكغ bashka*gh*, v. p.p. bashka*th*a, to give. P. ba*kh*shídan.

بشكغ bushka*gh*, v. p.p. bu*kh*tha, to discharge a gun.

بغا ba*gh*á, s. coward, runaway.

بغل ba*gh*l, s. in the phrase ba*gh*l gira*gh*, to embrace. Ar.

بغير ba*gh*air, except, without. Ar.

بكچي bukchí, horse's mane.

بكل bakkal, a Hindú, a trader. Ar. بقال.

بكهو bakhú, where?

بگ bag, a herd of camels. Panj. bag. Si. vagu.

بل bil, imperative of ila*gh*. Bil-dai! let go!

بل bal, spear.

بلا billá, s. medal.

بلرو balrú, infant.

بلكو balgo, dirt.

بلوغت balú*gh*at, puberty. Ar.

بلي billí, cat. Hindi, Si., Panj.

بن ban, exposed surface of a stratum of rock, sandstone.

بن bun, root, bottom. P.

بنا buná, below, at the bottom.

بند band, an embankment. P.

بندر bundar, the buttocks. Si. bunḍaṛu.

بندغ banda*gh*, v. p.p. bastha, to tie, bind. P. bastan.

Saren-banda*gh*, to help.

Dro*gh*-banda*gh*, to lie.

بنديخ bandí*kh*, thread.

بنغ buna*gh*, baggage.

بنو banú, an embankment round a field. Si. bano.

بني binni, a donkey's pack-saddle.

بنياد bunyád, foundation. P.

بو bo, s. smell. P.

Gand-bo, stink.

Náz-bo, pleasant smell.

بوت bot, vermin.

بوٹغ búṭa*gh*, v. p.p. búṭa*th*a, to close (the eyes).

بوٹغ bú*th*a*gh*, bracelet.

بوخته bo*kh*ta, p.p. of bozha*gh*. q. v.

بوڈ bo*dh*, a small tree producing Gúgal gum, *Balsamodendron mukul*.

بور bor, chestnut (of a horse); poetically a mare, horse Si. boru.

بور búr, a bud.

بورچي borchi, a cook. Turkish.

بوز boz, the Gúgal tree, also the drug obtained from it, *Balsamodendron mukul*. See bo*dh*.

بوز búz, wild, savage.

بوژغ bozha*gh*, p.p. bo*kh*tha, to open, untie. (Cf. pázand, bozheshn, release.)

بوژي bozhí, a boat. A.

بوغ bo*gh*, a joint in wood.

بوف bauf, a pillow, mattrass.

بوکغ boka*gh*, (1) to bleat as a goat; (2) to be proud, frisky.

بولک bolak, a tribe.

بولي búlí, beestings.

بولي bolí, speech.

بوهاري bohárí, sweeping. Si. buhárí.

بوهتار bohtár, a host, entertainer.

بوهري boharí, in front.

بوهل bohal, a barren, salt mountain.

بوهره bohra, a vault, cellar.

بها bhá, s. price. Si. bahá. bhá-gira*gh*, to buy.

بها bahá, v. the River Indus.

بهادر bahá*dh*ur, brave, a hero.

بهاگيا bhágyá, rich, well off. Si. bhágyo.

بهان bihán, a filly.

بهانڈا bhánḍá, a fold, enclosure, pen. Si. bhán*d*o.

بهاي baháí, sale.

بهت bhit, a wall. Si.

بهٹي bhaṭṭí, a kiln. Si.

بهر bahar, a share. P. Bahar-khana*gh*, to deal, divide.

بهرکها baharkhá, the month of Chait. P. bahár.

بهرغ bhura*gh*, p.p. bhuri*th*a, to be crushed, burst. Si. bhuraṇu

بهشت bihisht, heaven. P.

بهولو bholú, monkey. Si.

بهوريغ bhorena*gh*, v. to break, burst (transitive). Causal of bhura*gh*.

Chham bhorena*gh*, to wink.

Khond bhorena*gh*, to kneel.

بهيڈي bheḍí, s. the ankle. Si. bheḍí.

بے be, pr. without. P.

بے ایمان be-ímán, faithless.
بے ادب be-adab, rude.
بے ارام be-áráin, uneasy.
بے انساف be-insáf, unjust.
بے اکل be-akul, senseless.
بے اکلي be-akulí, senselessness.
بے پهاڈ be-phá*dh*, a snake, (lit. without feet).
بے دهان be-dihán, thoughtless.
بے سناتي be-sanátí, useless.
بے سیک be-sek, weak.
بے شک be-shak, doubtless.
بے شمار be-shumár, innumerable.
بے فهما be-fahmá, unintelligible.
بے کار be-kár, unoccupied.
بے گناه be-gunáh, innocent.
بے میار be-miyár, } shameless.
بے هیا be-hayá, }
بے وس be-was, helpless.
بي bai. Imperative.
بي bí, } 3rd pers. sing. fut. and subjunctive, } of bía*gh*. Cf. Pashto ví.
بیث bí*th*, }
بیڈه bí*th*a. Past Part.
بیر bair, revenge. Bair-gira*gh*, to take revenge.
بیري bairí, revenge, enmity.
بیراني beráni, harm, damage.
بیر کهنغ ber-khana*gh*, to surround, encompass.
بیرو دیئغ bero-dea*gh*, to turn back.
بیڑي beṛí, a boat. Si.
بیگاه begáh, s. evening. Begahá, in the evening. P.
بیلن bílan, s. the small intestines.
بیل bel, (1) a friend; (2) a hoe. Si.
بینغ bena*gh*, s. honey. Bena*gh*-mahisk, a bee. (Cf. P. angubín.) Pashto gabína.

بینگ bíng, dog. Bíng, the Dog, *i. e.*, the middle star of the three forming the tail of *Ursa Major*. See under Gu-ránd. Bíng-mahisk, a horsefly.

بیوان bewán, wilderness. P. bayábán.

بیوخ bío*kh*, possible. Bío*kh*-ne*n*, impossible. Noun of agency from bía*gh*.

بیئغ bía*gh* v. to be, become, p.p. bí*th*a.

Bía*gh*-rava*gh*, p.p. bí*th*o-shu*th*a, to become, to suffice.

پ P.

پاتار pátár, a hole dug for roasting meat over.

پارا párá, hog-deer. Si.

پارت párat, charge, entrusting, confidence. Si.

پارہ pára, quicksilver. Si.

پاڈ páḍ, root. Si.

پاسنا pásná, a night attack.

پاک pák, clean. P.

پاکرا pákrá, camel's riding-saddle. Si. pákhiro.

پالو pálo, frost. P.

پالینغ pálena*gh*, to strain, sift, winnow.

پانجالي pánjálí, yoke (of oxen). Si. panj.

پاینا páiná, lower, eastern. P.

پٹ paṭ, s. silk. Si.

پت pat, s. confidence, trust.

پٹ paṭ, s. a bare plain. Si.

پتافا patáfá, in the heat of the sun.

پتل pital, brass. Si.

پتنگ patang, s. a moth.

پٹساکھ paṭsákh, oath. Si.

پچل pachul, curtain or side walls of a Baloch hut.

پخت pu*kh*t, s. the Bhán tree *(Populus Euphratica)*. See phu*kh*t.

پرڈو paraḍḍav, s. } echo. Si. parláu.
پرلا parlá, s. }

پروتا parútá, adj. stale.

پزادغ pazáda*gh*, s. a step-son, (husband's son).

پشانگ pasháng, s. a wild man, savage, idiot.

پشي pashí, s. a berry.

پکر pakar, adj. necessary.

پلان palán, camel pack-saddle. Panj.

پلوتا palútá, curse.

پليثغ palí*th*a*gh*, s. (p. falíta). The slow-match of a matchlock.

پندغ pinda*gh*, to beg. Si. pinaṇu.

پندوخ pindo*kh*, beggar. Noun of agency from pinda*gh*.

پنور pa*n*war, (also much-panwar), the Pleiades.

پور por, s. a flood.

پورغ púra*gh*, v. to bury. Si. púranu.

پورياه poriyáh, wages. Si. porhyo.

پوست post, s. poppy. Post-ḍoḍá, poppy-heads.

پوشغ posha*gh*, to dress. P.

پوشينغ poshena*gh*, to clothe. (Causal of posha*gh*.)

پوگوخ pogo*kh*, the gullet.

پوه poh, understanding. (Pashto poh.)

پوه‌کهنغ poh-khana*gh*, v. to explain.

پوه‌بيئغ poh-bía*gh*, v. to understand.

پهه pha, prep. on, upon, among. P. ba. Pashto. pah. Pársí pa.
Pha-wa*th*á*n*, among themselves.

پهاذ phá*dh*, s. foot, leg. Demí-phá*dh*, forefoot.
Be-phá*dh*, footless; a snake.
P. páí. Z. pádha. Skr. páda.

پهاذآغ phá*dh*-á*gh*, to arise.

پهاذپهشت phá*dh*-phusht, instep.

پهاذگزار phá*dh*-guzár, shoes.

پهاذمچهه phá*dh*-muchh, ankle.

پهاذمردان phá*dh*-murdán, toe.

پهاذمُردانغ phá*dh*-murdána*gh*, toes.
پهاذنلي phá*dh*-nalí, shin.
پهاذي phá*dh*í, ring worn on a woman's toe.
پهاذغ phá*dh*a*gh*, wheel.
پهار phár, leisure.
پهارت phárat, charge. See *párat*. Si.
پهارپهغ phárphu*gh*, a tree, (*Tecoma undulata*).
پهاري phárí, last year. P. pár-sál.
پهاريز phárez, temperate. P. parhíz, safe.
پهاش phásh, bare; phásh-phá*dh*, barefoot.
پهاشن pháshan, the male már*kh*or. P. pázan.
پهاغ phá*gh*, turban. Met. The succession to a chiefship. Si. pág.
پهانزده phá*n*zdah, fifteen. P.
پهاهو pháho, hanging; a noose. Ṡi.
پهپهر phiphar, lungs, lights. Panj. Si. phiphiru.
پهٹ phuṭ, hair.
پهٹکي phiṭkí, alum. Si.
پهٹ phiṭ, prickly-heat.
پهٹر phuṭur, original, genuine, thorough.
پهٹغ phiṭa*gh*, to turn sour. Si. phiṭaṇu.
پهٹک phuṭak, short, stunted; a dwarf.
پهتريک phatrík, a bush, (*Grewia populifolia.*)
پهث phi*th*, father. P. pidar. Pahl. pid.
پهث پهيرو phi*th*-phírú, forefathers.
پهثي phi*th*í, other, another. (In Kachí.)
پهخت phu*kh*t. See pu*kh*t, (*Populus euphratica*).
پهجي phají, } with, in company with.
پهجيا phajyá, }
پهجياارغ phajyá-ara*gh*, to recognize.
پهدو phado, pocket.
پهدئيغ phadea*gh*, v. p.p. phadá*th*a, to run.
پهديما phadímá, adv. behind.

پهذا phadhá, afterwards.

پهذي phadhí, hinder, coming after.

پهر phar, prep. for, on account of.

پهر phar, a wing, feather. P. par.

پهر phur, full. P. pur.

پهرا pahrá, watch, guard.

پهراف phuráf, a young female camel up to 3 years old.

پهرامغ pharámagh, to deceive, deceit.

پهراون pahráwan, long coat. Si.

پهراه phráh, broad. P. farákh.

پهراهاذ phráhádh, } breadth.
پهراهي phráhí, }

پهرچهي pharchhe, why? on what account?

پهرز phurz, tinder. Si. purdu.

پهرشتغ phirishtagh, an angel. P. firishta.

پهرشغ phrushagh, p.p. phrushtha, to break, burst (intr.). Cf. P. fursúdan.

پهرمان pharmán, command. P. farmán.

پهرو phurú, a moth.

پهري phurí, a musquito or sand-fly.

پهروه phroh, grey.

پهري phurí, a drop. Si.

پهروه phroh, a plant, (*Sagaretia Theesans ?*).

پهرينغ phirenagh, v. p.p. phirentha, to throw, cast. Cf. P. paránídan, to cause to fly.

پهر phur, ashes.

پهزادغ phizádagh, step-son, (husband's son).

پهزم phazhm, wool. P. pashm.

پهس phas, a sheep or goat. Pashto psah.

پهسو phaso, answer. Pahl. pasukho.

پهيسپهيري phisphairí, two days before yesterday. P. pas + phairí q. v.

پهسغ phusagh, a son. P. pisar.

پهشت phusht, the back. P. pusht.

پہشتي phushtí, a chaddar or sheet for wearing.

پہشغ phashagh, v. p.p. phakká, to cook. P. pazídan and H. pakká.

پہشک phaskk, a woman's garment, boddice.

پہکا phakká, (1) ripe, cooked ; (2) a boil. H. pakká.

پہکي phakkí, anything reduced to powder, and taken down at a gulp with water.

پہگرغ phagaragh, to melt, thaw.

پہگين phagen, early in the morning. P. pagáh, dawn.

پہل phul, a flower. Si. Panj.

پہل puhal, a bridge. P. pul.

پہلاٹ phuláṭ, steel. P. púlád.

پہلغ phullagh, to rob, plunder, p.p. phullitha. Si. phuraṇu.

پہلکند phulkand, sugar.

پہلو phalo, direction, way, side. Si. palau, edge, border. Pashto, ditto.

پہلوا phalwá, in a direction.

پہلوه phulúh, nose-ring. Si. búlo.

پہلي phallí, section of a tribe.

پہلي pahlí, rib. P. pahlú.

پہلي phullí, the cap of a gun.

پہليثغ phalíthagh, match of a matchlock. P. palíta or falíta.

پہليت phalít, unclean. P. palíd or palíz.

پہمبلي phimblí, eyelash. Si. pimbiṇí.

پہناد pahnád, side, direction.

پہنال pahnál, flank.

پہنچ phanch, five. P. panj.

پہنجک phanjak, one-fifth. (The share of plunder due to a chief.)

پہنجاه phanjáh, fifty. P. panjáh.

پہنوال pahnwál, shepherd.

پہني phiṇí, calf of leg. Panj.

پہنير phaner, curds, cheese. P. panír.

پہنير پچ phanerpuch, rennet.

پهواد phawád, a mountain, a peak.

پهوپهي phúphí, paternal aunt. Si. H.

پهوڎ phod*h*, } there, thither.
پهوڎان phod*hán*,

پهوڎان‌ديمي phod*hán*-demí, the common white bindweed.

پهور phor, a pipe made of clay, or a leaf of phísh, *Chamærops ritchieana*, twisted spirally.

پهوست phost, poppy. P. post.

پهوغ pho*gh*, s. chaff. (Cf. P. púk).

پهوک phog, s. a bush, *Calligonum polygonoides*. Si. panj.

پهوگري phogrí, s. a goat given as wages to a goatherd.

پهول phol, s. search, enquiry, demand. Si.

پهول پهرس phol-phurs, s. questioning. Si. P.

پهول کهنغ phol-khana*gh*, v. to ask, demand.

پهولغ phola*gh*, v. to search for. Si. pholaṇu.

پهولوخ pholo*kh*, v. one who demands, a robber.

پهونز pho*nz*, s. nose. (Cf. Pashto, pazah. Brahoi, bámas.)

پهيدارغ phedára*gh*, v. p.p. phedáshta, to show.

پهيڎ phíd*h*, s. heel.

پهيڎ phed*h*, } here, hither.
پهيڎان phed*hán*,

پهيڎاغ phe*dhágh*, visible. P. paidá.

پهيڎاغين phe*dhághen*, is coming. See *ágh*.

پهيڎغ phí*dhagh*, a plant. A small species of *Euphorbia* found in the southern Sulaiman hills.

پهير phír, s. an old man; phírand, an old woman; adj. old. P. pír.

پهير phír, s. the jál tree, *Salvadora oleoides*. Si.

پهيراري phairárí, adv. the year before last. P. pírár-sál.

پهيرك phíruk, s. grandfather.

پهيري phírí, s. old age.

پهيري phairí, adv. the day before yesterday. P. parí-roz.

پهيسغ phísa*gh*, } a small plant. See پهيڎغ
پهيڎغ phí*dhagh*,

پهيش phísh, the dwarf palm, *Chamærops ritchieana.*
پهيش phesh, first, before. P. pesh.
پهيشي pheshí, adj. former, first.
پهيشا pheshá, formerly, first; pheshá, bundainagh, to forestall.
پهيغ phí*gh*, fat, grease. P. píh.
پهيفل phífal, a bush, *Daphne mucronata.*
پهيلا phílá, complete, full, perfect.
پهيمار phímáz, onion. P. piyáz.
پهيهغ pheha*gh*, to thrust; to enter forcibly. Si. pehaṇu.
پهيهي phehí, a scaffold (for watching crops). Si.
پياذغ piyá*dh*agh, a footman. P. piyáda.
پيثر pí*th*ar, a short grass found on the Sulaiman hills, growing between the coarse tufts or gasht.
پيچ pech, a screw. P.
پيدائيش paidáish, produce. P.
پيغام pai*gh*ám, a message. P.

ت T.

تابدار tábidár, obedient. A. P.
تاپهرغ táphura*gh*, v. p.p. táphuri*th*a, to stumble. Si. thábirjaṇu.
تاج táj, a cock's comb.
تار tár, wire. H.
تاري tárí, clapping of hands. Si. táṛí.
تازيم tázím, reverence. A.
تاس tás, cup. (Rare.)
تاككهفغ ták-khafa*gh*, to flinch, shy (of a horse).
تالابالا tálábálá, putting off, postponement. Si. ṭálo.
تالان tálan, a push. *Tálan* dea*gh*, to push.
تالو tálo, the palate. Si. tárú*n*.
تاه táh, odd (in numbers, as opposed to even).
تاهه táha, inside.
تاهث táha*th*, true, right, correct.

تبیت tabiyat, temper. A.

تپال tapál, post. Si. ṭapál.

تراتهه tráth, a plant (called *maitr* in the Deraját), *Anabasis multiflora.*

تران trán, counsel.

ترتهه tirtha, mad.

تروش trush, harsh, sour. P. tursh.

ترغ tara*gh*, v. p.p. tara*th*a, to swim. Si. taranu.

ترکغ tarka*gh*, p p. tarka*th*a, to cackle.

ترند trund, cruel, fierce, passionate.

ترهان tarhán, a young camel.

تري trí, an aunt (paternal). Panj. Skr. strí, woman.

تري زاخت trí-zá*kh*t, a cousin (paternal aunt's son).

ترير trer, dew. Si.

تریت trít, s. bread steeped in milk or soup.

تشنه tushna, s. frog.

تغار ta*gh*ár, a small watercourse on low hills.

تک tak. } See ták and ták-khafa*gh*.

تک کهفغ tap-khafa*gh*. }

تکا tikká, swift, sharp. Si.

تل tal, mole.

تلب talab, pay. A.

تلغ tala*gh*, v. to fry. Si. taranu.

تلي tillí, palm of hand ; sole of foot. Panj. tarí.

تماکو tamákú, tobacco.

تمبیلا tambelá, stable. A.

تمهو tumho, a plant, *Crotalaria Burhia.*

تنڈ tund, maimed. Si. ṭuḍo.

تنکه tankh, narrow. P. tang.

تنکه tankh, a pass through a defile. P.

تنگ tang, girth of a horse. P.

تنگ دیئغ ting-dea*gh*, to drink up.

تنگ tung, a hole. See ṭong.

تنگغ tanga*gh*, to hang. Si. ṭanganu.

توار tawár, voice, call, speech. Si.

توان tawán, a vessel for baking bread. P. tábá.

توان tawán, battle, fight (poet).

توبا tobá, a spring. Panj.

توپ top, a cap. Si. ṭopu.

توتا totá, parrot. P.

توخ to*kh*, a valley between two parallel ridges, a path through ditto.

توخ tau*kh*, voice, speech; tau*kh*-tawár, conversation.

توژ tauzh, adj. bitter, brackish.

توژ tauz*h*, s. a bush, *Salvadora Persica*.

توسغ tosa*gh*, v. See thosa*gh*.

توسينغ tosena*gh*, v. Causal of tosa*gh*.

توف tof, cannon. P. T. top.

توفک túfak, gun, matchlock. P. tufang.

توکل tawakkul, dependence, confidence. A.

تونگ tong, hole. See ṭong.

تهاخ thá*kh*, leaf.

تهار thár, dark. P. tár.

تهاف tháf, heat. P. táb.

تهاف tiháf, waterless. (P. tah, low and áb, water?).

تهافغ tháfa*gh*, oven. P. tábah.

تهاشغ thásha*gh*, p.p. thá*kh*tha, to gallop a horse. P. tá*kh*tan, táz.

تهاشي tháshí, s. gallopping; Galagh-thashí, horse-racing.

تهاله thála, s. a company.

تهان thá*n*, which? thángo, whither? thán-rangá, how?

تهان thá*n*, s. a pack-saddle.

تهانوان thá*n*wá*n*, s. damage.

تهپ thap, wound.

تهر thar, moist. P. tar.

تهرس thurs, thars, } fear. P. turs.

تهرسغ thursa*gh*, v. p.p. thursi*th*a, to fear. P. tursídan.

تھرسوخ thurso*kh*, a coward. Verbal noun from thursa*gh*.

تھرسینغ thursaina*gh*. Causal of thursa*gh*, to frighten.

تھرغ thara*gh*, to return; p.p. thar*th*a; thara*gh*-á*gh*, to come back.

تھرونگل throngal, hail.

تھرینغ tharaina*gh*. Causal of thara*gh*, to give back, send back.

تھسی thusí, a small bird.

تھسغ thusa*gh*, v. p.p. thustha, to faint; to go out (of a lamp).

تھش thash, an adze. P. tash.

تھشغ thasha*gh*, v. p.p. tha*kh*ta, to run, gallop. Zend. tach.

تھغار شور tha*gh*ársh0z, a plant.

تھغرد tha*gh*ard, matting made of the leaves of the phísh, (*Chamærops ritchiana*). Cf. Pashto ţa*gh*ar, carpet.

تھف fever, heat. P. tap.

تھفر thafar, an axe. P. tabar.

تھفغ thafa*gh*, to become hot.

تھل thal, a valley, an alluvial plain surrounded by hills.

تھل thul, a fort.

تھلانگ tahláng, face of an exposed rock-stratum.

تھلٹغ thalţa*gh*, v. to stammer.

تھلشک tahlishk, broken edge of an exposed rock-stratum.

تھم tham, ambush. Si.

Tham-bíagh, to lie in wait.

تھمت tuhmat, slander. A.

تھن thun, thirst.

تھنخ thana*kh*, thin, fine.

تھنگو thango, gold. P. tanka, tanga.

تھنی thuní, thirsty.

تھو thau, } thou, 2nd pers. pronoun sing. nom. P. tú. Pash-
تھہ tha, } to, tah.

تھورا thora, quarter (in fighting). Si.

تھوسغ thosa*gh*, v. p.p. thosta (causal of thusa*gh*), to extinguish, put out.

تھولغ thola*gh*, jackal.

تهولغ كنر tholagh-kunar, a bush, *Zizyphus oxyphylla.*

تهوم thom, garlic. Si. Panj. Ar. ثوم

تهي thí, other, another.

Thí-bare, another time, again.

Thí-roshe, another day.

Thí-kase, some one else.

Thí-bángá, day after to-morrow.

Thí-hande, somewhere else.

Thí-sál, next year.

تهير thír, bullet, arrow; thír-janagh, to shoot. P. tír.

تهيردان thír-dán, a bullet-pouch.

تهيرغ thíragh, horse's nose-bag.

تهيغ thegh, sharp, swift.

Thegháf, "swift water," name of a stream.

تهيغي theghí, all.

تهيل thíl, age (used of animals).

تهيلغ thelagh, eyeball.

تهوغين thewaghen, all, the whole.

تهيهه thíh, a slave (male).

تيربند tírband, the constellation Orion.

تيز tez, sharp. P.

تيژغ tezhagh, a melon.

تيژغي كهوه tezhaghí-khoh, a hone, whetstone.

تيلان telán, a push, shove. Si. thelho.

Telán deagh, to push.

ٹ Ṭ.

ٹبي ṭubí, advice. Si.

ٹپر ṭapur, felt, namda. Si.

ٹراما ṭrámá, copper. Si. ṭrámo.

ٹرپغ ṭrapagh, to drop, drip.

ٹرمغ ṭrimagh, to drip. Si. ṭrimanu.

ٹرموآف ṭrimu-áf, dripping well, or small waterfall.

ٹرکغ ṭraka*gh*, to burst (used of boils).

ٹروریڈار ṭroreḍár, a firelock.

ٹلو ṭilú, a bell.

ٹنڈني ṭinḍiní, firefly. Si.

ٹوبي ṭobí, dive. See ṭubí.

Ṭobí dea*gh*, to dive.

ٹوپو ṭopú, hat. Si. ṭopu.

ٹوند ṭond, turban, *met.* a great man.

ٹونگ ṭong, a hole. Si. ṭungu.

ٹھاھنغ ṭháhina*gh*, to make, construct. Si. ṭháhanu.

ٹھیڑ ṭheṛ, a mountain peak. Panj.

ٹھیٹھل ṭhíṭhal, female ravine deer.

ٹھیلغ ṭhíla*gh*, eyeball.

ٹیٹونا ṭíṭúná, the bulbul.

ٹیٹیھر ṭíṭíhar, the sand-piper, *Tringa goensis*.

ج J.

جابه jábah, quiver.

جار jár, net. Si. járu.

جار jár, twins. Si. jáṛo.

جاسوس jásús, spy. A.

جاغ já*gh*, v. p.p. jái*th*a, to chew.

جاگرو jágrú, watch. Si jágú.

Jágrú dára*gh*, to keep watch.

جام jám, chief. Si.

جان ján, body. P. ján, life.

ján-jebho, body armour.

ján-sho*dh*a*gh*, to bathe.

ján-khana*gh*, to dress.

جانگوه jángoh, arms and armour, when girt on the body.

جانور jánwar, domestic animals. P.

جاهل jáhil, lower, east. See jahl.

جائزو jáizo, promise, engagement. A. jáiz.

جت jat, camel-driver. Si.

جتهر jathir, millstone. Si. janḍru.

جثه ja*th*a, p.p. of jana*gh*.

جخت ju*kh*t, scabbard of a sword.

جغت ju*kh*t, adj. even (in numbers, as opposed to odd). Pashto ju*kh*t.

جر jar, clothes, dress.

جريده jarída, a poor man, pauper.

جزغ juza*gh*, to go, move.

gámá juza*gh*, to walk (of a horse).

جزوخ juzo*kh*. Verbal noun from juza*gh*, moving, the pulse.

جست jist, zinc. P.

جغدل ja*gh*dal, s. a Jaṭ.

جغدلي ja*gh*dalí, s. the language of the Jaṭs, viz., Panjábí or Sindhí.

جغر ja*gh*ar, liver. P. jigar.

جفت juft, a pair.

جلاه juláh, / جلوه juloh, } an attack. Si. julah.

جلگو julgav, a crowd.

جما jumá, Friday. Ar. jum'ah.

جمارا jamárá, everlastingly. Si. jamár.

جمب jumb, moving, shaking.

جمله jumla, collection, total, amount. Ar.

جن jan, s. woman. P. zan.

jan-gal, a band of women.

جنت jannat, / جنتل jantal, } heaven. Ar. جنت.

جنتهر janthir, / جندر jandar, } a mill, millstone. Si. janḍru.

جند jind, self, oneself. Si.

wa*th*í jinde*gh*en, one's own.

جنغ jana*gh*, v. p.p. ja*th*a, to strike. P. zadan, zan.

tárí jana*gh*, to clap hands.

chapol jana*gh*, to slap.

dápurá jana*gh*, to stamp.
di*gh*ár jana*gh*, to dig.
dafá jana*gh*, to boast.
dak jana*gh*, to solder.
dag jana*gh*, to rob on the highway.
dil jana*gh*, to vomit.
dang jana*gh*, to sting.
túfak jana*gh*, to shoot.
khátr jana*gh*, to breach a wall.
la*dh*a*gh* jana*gh*, to kick.
síndá jana*gh*, to whistle.
tau*kh* jana*gh*, to cry out.
go*gh*rá jana*gh*, to snore.
cháp jana*gh*, to clap hands.
gwánkh jana*gh*, to call out.

جنکه jinkh, janikh, } s. a daughter. Dim. of jan. Cf. Pashto jinaí, jínakaí.

جنگ jang, s. war. P. jung-bilá, a medal.

جو jo, s. a stream, canal. Pehl. jóí. P. júí.
syáh jo, a perennial stream.

جو jau, s. barley. P.

جواب jawáb, s. answer. A.

جوار jawár, s. a pair, yoke of oxen mate. Hind.

جواین jawái*n*, good.

جوانیا jawániyá, adv. well.

جوڈ jo*dh*, a man, warrior.

جور jor, adj. well, strong, in health. Si. joru.

جور jaur, poison.

جور jaur, the oleander, *Nerium oderum*.

جوژو jozho, a small fly.

جورغ joragh, جوریغ jorainagh, } to make, construct. Si. joṛanu.

جوغ jo*gh*, yoke. Si. jog.

جوفا júfá, avarice, usury, A. Si. jyáfa.

جوفاخور júfá*kh*or, a usurer.

جوگن jogin, a wooden mortar for cleaning corn.

جوگن دار jogindár, stick or pestal for ditto.

جول júl, a large bag.

جوهان jauhán, a heap of corn at harvest. P.

جهاتي jhátí, a peep. Si.

جهار jahár, s. a flock of birds. Si. jhári.

جهاز jaház, a ship. P.

جهان jihán, the world.

dehá jiháná, in the whole world.

جهپغ jhapa*gh*, to toss up. Si. jhapanu.

جهٹکغ jhaṭka*gh*, to sob. (Cf. Si. jhaṭko, a fit of passion.)

جهر jhur, clouds. Si. jhuṛu.

جهري jharí, of more than one colour.

جهگ jhag, foam, scum, froth, bubbles. Si.

جهل jhul, carpet. Si.

جهل juhul, deep.

جهل jahl, low.

جهلا jahlá, below.

جهل برز jahl-burz, ups and downs, inequalities.

جهلي jhallí, a pankha. Si.

جهن jhan, small bird (snipe?)

جهندا jhandá, a flag. Si.

جهيرا jhera, a quarrel, Si. jheṛo.

جيبهو jebho, s. armour.

جيت jait, camel-saddle.

جيدي jedí } (f.) a companion, associate.
جيدري jedirí }

جيڈ jí*dh*, s. pasture.

جيغ jí*gh*, s. bowstring. P. zih. Pushto, jaí. Si. jihu.

چ Ch.

چابر chábar, short grass.

چاپ cháp jana*gh*, to clap hands.

چاپول chápol jana*gh*, to slap.
چاث chá*th*, a well. P. cháh.
چارغ chára*gh*, v. p.p. chári*th*a, to look out, spy.
چاري chárí, a guide, spy. Si.
چاڑي cháṛí ascent, Si. chaṛhí.
چاک chák-dea*gh*, to split, rip up. P.
چاؤت cháút, threshold. Si. cháu*n*ṭhí.
چبهه chabha, sandals.
چپ کهنغ chup khana*gh*, to be quiet. Si.
چپ chap, left. P.
چپدست chap-dust, left hand. P.
چپحوت chap-chot, crooked.
چپاروي chaprúí, an English rupee.
چپي chapí, adj. left, sinister, unlucky.
چت chit, woman's petticoat.
چت chat, roof. H.
چتاکهنغ chatá khana*gh*, to grasp, catch hold of with the arms.
چتر chitar, matting.
چٹغ chaṭa*gh*, p.p. chaṭ*th*a, to lick. Si. Chaṭanu. Lab chaṭa*gh*, to flash in the pan.
چٹي chaṭí, s. a fine. Si.
چچهو chachho, how?
چر char, a path hemmed in by precipices on each side.
چر chur, a small hill torrent.
چرپ charp, adj. fat. P.
چرپي charpí, s. fat, grease.
چرز charaz, the houbara, *(otis houbara)*. P.
چرغ chara*gh*, to wander, go about. Si. charanu.
چرنگ chiring, s. a spark. Si. chiṇig.
چرو charo, merely, only.
چروخ charo*kh*, wanderer, vagabond.
چرهٔ chirra, shot.
چرينغ charaina*gh*, to watch cattle, to graze. Causal of chara*gh*.

چري charí, madman.
چڙغ charagh, to ascend, climb. Si. charhanu.
چشمه chushma, a spring. P. chashma.
چشغ chishagh, p.p. chishatha, to sneeze.
چغرد chighird, the bábul bush, (*Acacia Jacquemontii*).
چغل chughal, a spy.
چغل ديئغ chaghal deagh, to throw away.
چكتر chiktar, } how much? How many? (Probably for chi
چكر chikar, } qadr).
چكغ chikagh, to pull, drag. Si. chhikanu.
چكغ chukagh, to kiss.
چكهه chukh, a child.
چكهه چوري chukhchorí, children.
چكههه chakha, on, upon.
چگا chagá, testing. Chagá-hálwar, a laughing matter.
چل chil, forty. P. chihal.
چلغ chillagh, to peel, scrape. P. chalídan.
چلر chillur, peel, bark, scales.
چلكغ chilkagh, to shine, glitter. Si. chilkanu.
چلگذغ chalgudhagh, bat.
چلمب chulumb, s. earring. (Cf. Si. chumbulu.)
چلو chalo, s. a ring. Si. chhalo.
چمب chamb, a spring.
چمبرغ chambaragh, v. p.p. chambaritha, to spring upon. Si. chambaranu.
چمبو chambo, ball of foot, claw. Si.
چمرڙ chamra, bat. Si. chamiro.
چمغ chamagh, a spring, fountain. P. chashma. See chhamagh.
چنا chaná, opinion. (Cf. P. chanídan.) Maín chaná, in my opinion.
چنجو chinjú, crowbar.
چنڈ chund, } point of the compass.
چنڈرا chundrá, }
چنغ chinagh, p.p. chitha, to pick up, gather, collect. P. chídan.

چنگ chang, banjo or guitar. B.

چوت chot, adj. crooked, bent.

Chot khana*gh*, to bend, tr.
Chot bía*gh*, to bend, intr.
Chot chham, squinting.

چوٹو choṭo, a horse-fly.

چوا chawá, jest.

چواگر chawágar, jester.

چوچ chúch, little finger. Si. chích.

چوپہير chaupher, round.

چورو choro, boy. Panj.

چوري chorí, orphan. Si. chhoro.

چوري chúrí, chicken.

چوفغ chofa*gh*, v. p.p. chofi*th*a, to pound, thump. (Cf. P. koftan).

چہاث chha*th*, a well. P. cháh. Z. chittha, pit.

چہہ chih, what?

چہل chhil, forty. P. chihal.

چہلو chhilav, cold weather (Jan. Feb.).

چہم chham, the eye. P. chashm.

chham bhoraina*gh*, to wink.
chham phusht, eyelid.

چہتر chhatar, s. joke.

چي chí for هيچي hechí, anything. P.

چي chí, s. a thing; chíe-chíe, somewhat.

چيار chyár, four; yake chyár, fourfold. P. chahár.

chyár gíst, 80; chyár kund, four-conered.
chyár gíst dah, 90.
chyár phá*dh*, foor-footed.

چيارده chyárdah, fourteen.

چيارمي chyáramí, fourth.

چيبر chebar, news.

چيت آرغ chít ára*gh*, to be crushed. Si. chitáranu.

چيتغ cheta*gh*, to repair, mend. Si. chetanu.

چیذغ chedhagh, a cairn erected to commemorate any notable event.
چیکلو chiklo, a little.

خ Kh.

خازگ *kh*ázg, dirt.
خازگ بروخ *kh*ázg-barokh, sweeper.
خازگو *kh*ázgo, dirty.
خان *kh*áṇ, chief. See Hán.
خاندان *kh*ándán, family.
خدمت *kh*idmat or *kh*izmat, service.
خر *kh*ar, a donkey (female).
خرگوشک *kh*argoshk, a hare.
خرچ *kh*arch, expenses.
خمیس *kh*amís, Thursday.
خندغ *kh*anda*gh*, p.p. *kh*andi*th*a, to laugh. Su khanda*gh*.
خوجا *kh*ojá, eunuch.
خوش *kh*ush, happy. See wash.
خوشي *kh*ushí, happiness.

د D.

داپرا dápurá jana*gh*, to stamp. Si. dáphoṛá.
داث گپت dá*th*gipt, dealings.
دار dár, wood.
دارغ dára*gh*, v. p.p. dáshta, to have, hold, hold in. dáshtiyá quietly! P. dáshtan, dár.
داس dás, a grass-knife; sickle.
داغ dágh, داغان dá*gh*án, } brand, spots, blemishes. P.
دالا dálá, thick.
دان dán, corn. P. dána.

دانا dáná,
دانکوه dánkoh,
داني dání, } until, up till, till when. (Cf. Si. dání, time.)
داهنتهي dáhanthí,
دائين dáin,

داهن dáhn, complaint. Si. dánh.

داي dáí, nurse. P.

دائيمه dáima, for ever. A.

داواگر dáwágar, s. champion.

دتهان dathán, s. tooth. P. dandán.
dathán-dor, toothache.

دخ di*kh*, s. spindle. P. dúk.

دذغ di*dh*a*gh*, p.p. da*kh*ta, to brand.

در dar, prep. out, outside. (P. dar, door.)

دربرغ dar-bara*gh*, to defend.

درکهفغ dar-khafa*gh*,
درآغ dar-á*gh*, } to come out.

درروغ dar-rava*gh*,
درشفغ dar-shafa*gh*, } to escape.

درکهنغ dar-khana*gh*, to put out, expel.

درسرغ dar-sara*gh*, to protect.

درگيژغ dargezha*gh*, to look out.

درا dará, adv. outside.

دراخ drá*kh*, s. vine. Si. ḍrákh.

دراژ drázh, adj. long. P. daráz.

دراژاذ drázhá*dh*,
دراژي drázhí, } s. length.

دراه duráh, well, in health.

دراهي duráhí, health.

دراهيا daráhiyá, a promise.

در durr, good, excellent.

در durr, an earring worn in the lobe of the ear (P. durr, pearl).

درجغ dirja*gh*, see dina*gh*, to burst.

درد dard, pain. P.

درست drust, all, the whole. (Pashto drast.)

درشغ drisha*gh*, p.p. drishtha, to bite.

درشغ drusha*gh*, p.p. drushtha, to grind.

درشک darashk, tree. P. dira*kh*t.

درغ diragh. See dina*gh*, to tear. P. darídan.

درمان darmán, s. medicine, spirits, gunpowder. P. dárú, darmán.

درنزغ dra*n*za*gh*, to go swiftly (poet).

درنگ drang, precipice.

دروشم drosham, front, foremost part, shape, countenance.

دروغ dro*gh*, false. P.

dro*gh*-banda*gh*, to lie.

dro*gh*-bando*kh*, liar.

دروغ وند dro*gh*vand, lying, deceit.

دروه droh, false. Si.

دره drub, all.

درهاني druháni, pistol.

دري darrí, out, outwards.

دريس drís, a Baloch dance, at weddings, and also (called *jhamar*,) rejoicings, accompained with shouting or groaning.

درين drín, rainbow.

دز duz, thief. P. duzd.

دزغ duza*gh*, to steal. P.

دزواگ daz-wág, bridle. (For dast-wág.)

دزواهي duzwáhí, friendship.

دزي duzí, theft. P.

دژک dazhak, s. a snipe.

دژمن duzhman, enemy. P. dushman.

Cf. Zend. duzh, in duzhda, evil, &c.

دژمني duzhmaní, enmity. P.

دست dast, s. hand. P.

dast-á*gh*, dast-khafa*gh*, } to get, obtain, come to hand.

dast-láina*gh*, to touch.

dast-laṭh, walking-stick.

dast-*kh*att, signature.

دستغ dasta*gh*, handle. P. dasta.
دستور dastúr, custom. P.
دشت dasht, a barren plain or tableland. P.
دعا du'á, prayer. A.
ne*kh*-du'á, blessing.
bad-du'á, curse.
دغار di*gh*ár, land, ground, level country. P. díhár.
di*gh*ár-wázhá, landlord.
di*gh*ár-jana*gh*, to dig the ground.
دف daf, s. mouth.
daf-jana*gh*, to boast.
daf-dáragh, to be silent.
dafá-dár ! be silent !
دفار dafár, } mouthful.
دوار dawár, }
دفتر daftar, } bard. P.
دوتر davtar, }
دفسر dafsar, cover, lid.
دک dak, join, mending.
دك جنغ dakjana*gh*, to solder.
دکهه dukh, needle's eye.
دکهه dukh, trouble. Si.
دکهیا dukhyá, with difficulty.
دگ dag, road. Si. dagu.
dag-jana*gh*, to rob on the highway.
دگو duggav, s. eagle.
دل dil, s. heart, zeal. P.
dil-jana*gh*, to retch.
dil-shu*th*í, retching.
dil-gír, sorrowful.
دلغ dala*gh*, s. boiled rice.
دلکودئیغ dalko-dea*gh*, to threaten.
دلو dillo, an earthenpot, ghaṛá. Si. dilo.
دمب dumb, tail. P. dum.
mazár-dumb, tiger's-tail (a plant).

دمبیرو dambíro, a Baloch banjo or guitar.

دمبل dambul, a cairn erected in irony to commemorate a shameful action. P.

دن dan, a tax levied by Baloch chiefs. See ḍan.

دنانکرا daná*n*kará, till then.

دنغ dina*gh*,
درغ dira*gh*, } p.p. dirtha, to tear. P. darídan, din.
درجغ dirja*gh*,

دنز da*n*z, dust. (Cf. Si. daj.)

دنیکر daníkar, till now.

دنیا dunyá, the world, people. A.

دو do, two. P.

دوگیست do-gíst, forty. See chil.

دوار dawár. See dafár.

دوازده dwázdah, twelve. P.

دوازدمي dwázdamí, twelfth.

دوبر dobar, the chest.

دوبران dobarán, twice.

دوتر davtar, bard, reciter of genealogies. P. daftar.

دور dor, pain. { dathán-dor, tooth-ache.
láf-dor, belly-ache.

دور daur, rich.

دورا dorá, double. Si. duhuro.

دوروخ doro*kh*, ill, in trouble or pain.

دوزخ doza*kh*,
دوژي dozhí, } hell. P. doza*kh*. Z. duzha*n*ha. Pashto dozha*kh*.

دوست dost, friend. P.

دوشغ dosha*gh*, p.p. dokhtha, to sew. P.

دوشغ dosha*gh*, p.p. dushtha, to milk. P.

دوشي doshí, last night. P.

دوغ do*gh*, p.p. do*th*a, to fetch water.

دوغین do*gh*ín, pregnant.

دولت daulat, wealth. A.

دومنديل dúmandíl, with two turbans, *i. e.*, a man of distinction.
درهون dúho*n*, smoke. Si.
ده dah, ten. P.
دهان dihán, thought, consideration. Si. dhyánu.
دهک dhak, hurt, injury. Si. dhaku.
دهغ daha*gh*, to get, touch.
دهل dhul, drum. Panj. ḍhol.
دهمي dahmí, tenth.
دهنگ dhing, powerful.
دهور dhúr, dust. Si. dhúri.
دهوس dahús, bastard, a term of abuse.
دهوليا dhúliyá, dust. Si.
دي dí, also. Dí—dí. Both—and.
ديب deb, thumb.
ديڈلو dí*th*lo, mist. (P. dúd, smoke.)
ديخ dí*kh*, spindle. P. dúk.
ديذ de*dh*, an earthen pot. See dez.
ديذ dí*dh*, } sight. P. dídár, díd.
ديذار dí*dh*ár, }
ديدوخ dído*kh*, eyeball.
دير dír, far, apart, separate. P. dúr.
dír-zána*gh*, far-seeing, wise.
دير der, while, time. P. der.
ديز dez, pot.
ديغرا de*gh*rá, large pot. P.
ديم dem, face. P. adíma. Z. daema.
ديما demá, before, in front.
ديم dím, back.
ديما dímá, behind.
ديه deh, country, land, tract, territory. Si. ḍehu. P. deh.
Z. da*n*ha. Skr. deśa.
ديئغ dea*gh*, v. p.p. dá*th*a, to give. P. dádan.
dem-dea*gh*, to send.
drik-dea*gh*, to leap.

ila*gh*-dea*gh*, to let go.
sar-dea*gh*, to send away.
gon-dea*gh*, to accompany.
má*n*-dea*gh*, to apply.
mokal-dea*gh*, to dismiss.

ڈ Ḍ.

ڈاٹو ḍáṭo, dust.
ڈاچي ḍáchí, a female camel. Si.
ڈاڈي ḍáḍí, grandmother. Si.
ڈاڈي پوتري ḍáḍepotre, descendants of the same ancestor. Si.
ڈان ḍán, desert.
ڈانڈالي ḍándálí, a winnowing-sieve.
ڈاني ḍání, time, a certain time. Si.
ڈاہ ḍáh, alarm, war news. Si.
ڈڈ ḍid,
ڈڈر ḍiḍar, } frog. Si. ḍeḍaru.
ڈڈو ḍaḍḍav, pony, nag. Si. ḍraḍro.
ڈرتغ ḍratta*gh*, v., p.p. ḍratta*th*a, to fall. Si. ḍrahanu, p.p. ḍraṭho.
ڈرك ḍrik, jump, spring.
ڈركغ ḍrika*gh*, to jump.
ڈركان ḍrakán, carpenter. Si. ḍrakhanu.
ڈرگغ ḍraga*gh*, to canter. (Si. ḍrak).
ڈروہ ḍroh, falsehood, lie. Si.
ڈروھا ḍrohá, false, dishonest.
ڈسغ ḍasa*gh*, v., p.p. dasa*th*a, to show, point out. Si. ḍasanu.
ڈكال ḍukál, dearth, famine. Si. ḍukáru.
ڈگھ ḍigh, pice, copper coin.
ڈن ḍan, by force, violently. Si. ḍanu.
ڈنپھور ḍanphúr, a forcible contribution.
ڈندور ḍandwar, a tooth-brush.
ڈنگ ḍang, sting. Si. ḍangu.
ḍang-jana*gh*, to sting.
ڈوڈا ḍoḍá, poppy-heads.

ڈڈ ḍoḍ, framework, bones. Panj.

hushke*n* ḍoḍ, a dry skeleton.

ڈور ḍor, a pond. Si. ḍhoro.

ڈول ḍol, a bucket. Si. ḍolu.

ڈولا ḍaulá, the forearm. Si. ḍoro.

ڈولو ḍolo, cooked.

ḍolo bia*gh*, to be crooked.

ڈوم ḍom, / ڈومب ḍomb, } bard, minstrel. Si.

ḍombáṇí-áf, / ḍomb-khushta*gh*, } mirage (connected with a legend of a minstrel's death).

ڈونگ ḍong, bottle.

ڈونگا ḍúngá, deep. Panj.

ڈوه ḍoh, sin, offence. Si. dohu.

ڈوي ḍoí, spoon. Si.

ڈهابرغ ḍhábura*gh*, p p. ḍháburtha, to stumb.

ڈهال ḍhál, shield. Si. Panj.

ڈهکن ḍhakan, cover. Si.

ڈهکني ḍhakaní, knee-pan. Si. ḍhakiṇí.

ڈهونڈ ḍhúnḍ, skeleton. Si.

ڈهينگ ḍhíng, crane.

ڈيڈر ḍíḍar, muscles, biceps.

ڈير ḍer, husband's younger brother. Si. ḍeru.

ڈير ḍír, / ڈيل ḍíl, } body, form, shape. Si. ḍílu.

ڈيلهو ḍelhú, fruit of the khaler (*capparis aphylla*). Si. ḍelho.

ڈيمبهو ḍembhú, wasp. Si.

ڈيو ḍío, lamp. Si. ḍio.

ڈيهو ḍíhav, leopard.

ر R.

راچي ráchí, camel-driver.

رازا rázá, painter.

راست rást, true. P.

راستي rástí, truth. P.

راك rák, cheek-bone.

ران rán, thigh. P.

راه ráh, road. P.

راهدي ráhdí, fate, death.

راهزن ráhzan, head of a band of robbers. P.

راهک ráhak, cultivator. Panj.

رب rabb, God. A.

رپته rapta, p.p. of rava*gh*, used in the sense of began, begun; its place in the meaning went, gone being supplied by shu*th*a. P.

رخته ri*kh*ta, p.p. of rísha*gh*. q. v.

رڈ riḍ, f. sheep (small-tailed). Si. riḍh.

ذغ ra*dh*a*gh*, p.p. rastha, to tear up the ground.

رذغ ra*dh*a*gh*, to be beaten, to lose (in war or play).

رذغ ru*dh*a*gh*, v. p.p. rustha, to grow, germinate, spring up mount. P. rustan.

رزينغ razaina*gh*, p.p. razaintha, to make.

رس ras, juice, sap. Si. rasu.

رستر rastar, wild beasts, game.

syáhe*n* rastar, wild swine.

رسغ rasa*gh*, p.p. rasi*th*a, to arrive. P. rasídan.

رسينغ rasaina*gh*. Causal of rasa*gh*.

رشک rashk, lice.

رغ ra*gh*, pulse. P. rag, vein.

رغام ra*gh*ám, collection of clouds, threatening weather.

رفتار raftár, paces. P.

رکهه rakh, s. lip.

رکيب rikeb, stirrup. P. rikáb.

رگ rag, vein, pulse. See ra*gh*.

رگ rug, precipice.

رلغ rala*gh*, to mix, join. Si. ralanu.

رمب rumb, a run.

rumb zíra*gh*, to run, hurry.

رمبغ rumba*gh*, to run away, gallop, race (on foot).

رمبہ ramba, chisel. Si. rambo.

رمال rumál, towel. P.

رمغ rama*gh*, flock of goats. P. ramah.

رن ran, married woman. Panj. ranḍ.

رند rand, track, path. Si. randu.

sar-rand, comb.

رندغ randa*gh*, to comb, part the hair.

رنغ runa*gh*, p.p. rutha, to reap. Cf. Pashto, ravdal. Skr. lú.

رو ro, contracted from ro*th*, 3rd per. aor. of rava*gh*, will go, goes, may go.

رو ro, contraction for rosh, day, sun.

har-ro, every day, always.

ro-táf, heat of sun, glare.

روپہسک rophask, s. a fox (uncommon). P. rúbáh.

روپہغ ropha*gh*, a loud noise.

روبرو rúbarú, in the presence of. P.

روث ro*th*, entrails. P. rúda.

رودار rodár, bowstring, fiddlestring.

روذ ro*dh*, high bank of a torrent or stream. P. rúd.

روذغ ro*dh*a*gh*. See ru*dh*a*gh*.

روذن ro*dh*in, madder.

روذینغ ro*dh*aina*gh*, to bring up, educate.

روڑ roṛ, calf.

roṛ-gal, herd of calves.

روژگیر rozh-gír, eclipse of the sun (from rosh and gira*gh*).

روش rosh, day, sun. P. roz.

rosh-ásán, sunrise.

rosh-er-shaf, sunset.

rosh-tiká, daybreak.

roshe-roshe, day by day.

roshe-veláe, from time to time.

روشغ roshag*h*, a fast. P. roza.

روغن rog*h*an, clarified butter, ghí. P.

روغ ravagh, p.p. shu*th*a, to go. P. raftan, shuda.

dar-ravag*h*, to escape.

mán-ravag*h*, to enter.

bíag*h*-ravag*h*, to become.

روفرو rofro, a fox. P. rúbáh.

روکهنغ rokhanag*h*, v., p.p. rokhu*th*a, to light, kindle.

رومست romast, chewing the cud.

رونگرا rúngrá, a narrow hill path.

روه rúh, soul. A. rúḥ.

ره rah, edge, edge of knife.

رهنغ rahnag*h*, edge or bank of river.

ریبند ríband, fringe or horse's forehead.

ریت rít, custom. Si. ríti.

ریخ re*kh*, sand. P. reg.

sar-re*kh*, cold in the head.

ریر rer, } rags.
ریل ríl, }

ریز rez, a rope (made of cotton thread).

ریزم rezam, blight (of corn).

ریسغ resag*h*, p.p. restha, to spin, twist. Pashto reshal.

ریسنغ resinag*h*, to pursue, chase; p.p. resintha.

ریش rísh, beard. P.

ریش resh, gall (on the back of a horse or beast of burden).

ریشغ ríshag*h*, p.p. ri*kh*tha, to pour, spill, scatter, sow (seed).

P. rí*kh*tan.

ریشینغ ríshainag*h*. Causal of ríshag*h*.

ریم rem, grass.

ریم rem, matter, pus. P. rím.

ریئغ ríag*h*, cacare.

ز Z.

زا zá, abuse, bad language.

زات zát, tribe, caste. A.

زات zát, coloured cloth.

زاخت zá*kh*t, son (in composition). P. záda. Skr. játa.

ná*kh*ozá*kh*t, nephew (son of paternal uncle).

trízá*kh*t, nephew (son of paternal aunt).

wasarzá*kh*t, brother-in-law.

زاد zád, many-coloured, variegated.

زاغ zá*gh*, v. p.p. zá*th*a, to give birth, bring forth. P. zádan.

زال zál, woman. P.

زاماث zámá*th*, son-in-law. P. dámád. Skr. jámátṛi. Pashto zúm.

زامر zámur, s. name of a tree.

زامن zámin, surety. A.

زامن گیري zámingírí, bail, security.

زان zán, thigh.

زانتهو zántho, a., p.p. of zána*gh*, knowingly.

زانغ zána*gh*, p.p. zántha, to know. P. dánistan. Z. zná. Skr. jná.

زانمر zá*n*mur. See zámur.

زايفه záifa, a woman. A.

زخم zá*kh*m, a wound. P.

زذغ za*dh*a*gh*, wounded. (P. zada.)

زر zar, money. P.

زراغ zará*gh*, leech. (Si. jaru.)

زرتهه zurth, jowar. (Cf. Pehl. júrḍák, corn.)

زرد zard, yellow. P.

زردو zardo, yolk of an egg.

زردوي zardoí, bile.

زردي zirde, heart (poet.) Skr. hridi. Zend. zaredhaya. Pashto zṛah.

زرور zarúr, necessary. A.

زره zirih, armour. P.

زره zirih, a well.

زغر zaghar, adj. fresh, quick.

zagharen shír, fresh milk.

زك zik, a bag or "maskína" for holding ghí. (Si. jik. Pashto zik).

زمستان zamistán. See zawistán, winter. P.

زناخ zanákh, jaws. (P. zanakh, chin.)

زناور zanáwar, animal. P. jánwar.

زنجير zanjír, chain. P.

زندغ zindagh, living. P. zinda.

زنغ zinagh, v., p.p. zitha, zintha or zítha, to snatch, take away forcibly.

زنگ zang, s. turnip.

زنگ zang, } rust.
زنگال zangál, }

زور zor, force, might, violence, wrong. P.

زور zivir, rough, not smooth. (Cf. Pashto zig.)

زوراخ zorákh, powerful, violent.

زوروالا zorwálá, oppressor, tyrant.

زواذ zawádh, scent, smell. P. zabád.

زوار zawár, pebbles.

زوار zawár, rider, horseman. (P. sawár).

زوال zawál, s. injury.

زوان zawán, tongue. P. zabán.

زوستان zawistán, winter. P. zamistán.

زه zah, kid.

zah-gal, flock of kids.

زهر zahr, anger. P.

zahr-giragh, to be angry.

زهر zahr, bitter.

زهرك zahrak, the gall-bladder. P. zahra.

زهم zahm, sword.

zahm-band, swordbelt.

zahm-jano*kh*, swordsman.

zahm-band, scar of a sword wound.

زهیر zahír, lonely, a stranger. A.

زي zí, yesterday. P. dí-rúz.

زیاني ziyání, harm, injury. Pehl. ziyán.

زیارت ziyárat, shrine, place of pilgrimage. A.

زیث zí*th*, quick. P. zúd.

زیثین zí*th*en, quickly.

زیخا zai*kh*á, s. ferns, moss, &c.

زیرغ zíra*gh*, v. p.p. zurtha, to raise, lift.

zíra*gh*-ára*gh*, to fetch.

lashkar zíra*gh*, to lead an army.

sáh zíra*gh*, to draw breath.

rumb zíra*gh*, to run, sau*gh*an zíra*gh*, to swear.

زیم zím, scorpion.

زین zen, saddle. P. zín.

zen-kana*gh*, to saddle.

ژ Zh.

ژانگغ zhánga*gh*, v. to bray.

ژلوخ zhalo*kh*, adj. yellow.

ژله دیئغ zhala dea*gh*, v. to let go. (See ila*gh*.)

ژمارا zhamárá, for ever. See jamárá.

ژنگہه کهنغ zhinga khana*gh*, to erect the tail (of a horse).

ژنگ zhing, adj. erect, perpendicular. Also the name of a Baloch sub-tribe.

س S.

سابون sábún, soap. Portuguese. Ar.

ساتهه sáth, a káfila. Si. sáthu.

ساد sád, honest. (P. sádá, plain (?)).

ساڈ sá*dh*, rope (of múnj or dwarf-palm leaves).

سارتهه sárth, cold. P. sard.

ساري sári, rice growing or in husk. P. shálí.

ساز sáz-kana*gh*, to play (a musical instrument).

ساكهه sákh, oath. Si.

ساگ ság, potherb. Si.

ساگي sági, that very one, the original. Si.

سال sál, a year. P.

سالغ sála*gh*, parched corn.

سالوخ sálo*kh*, bridegroom.

سامبغ sámba*gh*, to favour, nourish. Si. sámbhanu.

سان sán, stallion, bull. Si. sánu.

سانگ sáng, betrothal. Si. sangu.

سانگي sángí, spear. Si. sángi.

ساه sáh, shade. P. sáya.

ساه sáh, breath, life. P.

sáh-zíra*gh*, to breathe.

ساهدار sáhdár, domestic animals.

ساهي sáhí, a pause, breathing space, fallow.

sáhí-dea*gh*, to let land lie fallow.

ساين sái*n*, sir, master. Si. Skr. swámi.

ساينغ sáina*gh*, v., p.p. sáintha, to shave.

Imperative, sá, sará sa, shave the head.

سبي subí, autumn.

سپي sippí, shell. Si.

ستة sath, a deputation to ask pardon.

ستي sutí, a musquito.

سجي sijjí, roast meat.

سخ si*kh*, barren land.

سدها sidhá, straight. Si. sidho.

سڈكغ suḍka*gh*, to sob. Si. suḍikanu.

سده sudh, } knowledge, understanding. Si. sudhi. Pashto sud.

سذ su*dh*, }

سذ sa*dh*, a hundred. P. sad.

سر sar, a man. Pashto, saṛai.

سر sar, s. head, front. P.

sar-gira*gh*, to set out.

sar-dea*gh*, to send away.

سردر sar-dar, bareheaded. (Pashto, saḍar.)

سردار sar-dár, } s. chief.
سردر sar-dar, }

سرپوس sarposh, covering.

سرریخ sar-re*kh*, cold in the head.

سررند sar-rand, parting of hair.

سرناوغ sar-náva*gh*, the morning star (poet.).

سرا sará, adv. and prep. above, upon, ahead, in front.

sará-bai, go in front.

سرايرا sará-era, adv. from above, downwards.

سربري sarbarí, upper.

sarbarí-pahná*dh*á, on the upper side.

سرپهڈ surpha*dh*, } s. (Ar. سرفت), understanding.
سرپهو surpho, }

surpha*dh* bía*gh*, to understand.

سرجه sarjah, pillow.

سرساد sursád, provisions, forage. Si. sursát.

سرغ sara*gh*, p.p. sari*th*a, to remember.

سرغ sira*gh*, to leap, prance. Si. siranu.

سرغ sura*gh*, to move. Si. suranu.

سرکهه sarakh, a kneading-trough.

سرگو surgo, speech, song.

سرل saral, a yearling colt. Si. sarlu.

سرم surum, hoof. P. sum.

سرنگ saring, a track. Si. suringh.

saring-jana*gh*, to track.

سري sarí, a woman's chadar.

سرين saren, loins.

saren-banda*gh*, to gird up the loins, help.

saren-bandí, assistance.

سريندا saríndá, } s. a sort of fiddle with seven strings of sheep's
سرندو sarindo, } gut played with a horsehair bow. Si. surundo.

سرینه sarína, upper; western. P.

سروذ sarodh, music.

سروش sarosh, elbow.

سڑک saṛak, road. Hindí.

سزا sazá, punishment. P.

سستي sustí. See sutí.

سشغ sushagh, p.p. sukhtha, to burn. (Intransitive.)

سغار saghár, adj. white-faced (of a horse).

سغدتا saghdattá, a small thorny plant.

سغر saghar, head.

سغرکهه sagharkha, a wild species of sinapis.

سغن saghan, dung of cattle.

سغندان saghindán, paunch, stomach.

سک sak, strong, stiff, hard. P. sakht.

سکتر sakatar, a kind of partridge.

سکل sakal, beautiful.

سکمردي sakmardí, manliness, strength.

سکني sakaní, Wednesday.

سکهغ sikhagh, to learn. Si. Sikhanu.

سکهينغ sikhainagh, to teach. Causal of sikhagh.

سکي saki, extreme, excess.

سکيا sakyá, } very, extremely.
سکيغا sakíghá, }

سگ sag, skill, ability. Si. sagh.

سل sil, brick. Si. sir. Panj. sil.

سلبند silband, brick-maker. Panj.

سلام salám, salutation.

salám-alaik, (Ar. سالم العايک), salutation on meeting.

سلهي silhe, arms. A. salaḥ.

silhe-gal, arms and accoutrements.

سما samá, understanding. Si. samáu.

سمب samb, a hole, boring.

sumb-janagh, to bore.

سمبراي sambaráí, preparation, readiness.

سمبرغ sambara*gh*, to prepare, be ready. Si. sambhiranu.

سمبغ sumba*gh*, stitch in the side.

سمندر samundar, sea.

سند sand, barren (of offspring). Pashto shanḍ. Si. shanḍhi.

سند sand, a joint. Si. sandhu.

سند sund, a basket of matting. Si. sundu.

سندان sindán, anvil.

سندغ sinda*gh*, v. p.p. sistha, to break.
P. shikastan, shikan.

سنج sanj, harness. Si. sanju.
sanj-khana*gh*, to saddle, harness.

سنگ sang, stone (uncommon). P.

سنگبند sangband, related by marriage (used of two tribes).

سنگتي sangatí, companions, following. Si.

سنگد sangad, companions, escort.

سني saní, hemp. Si. siṇí.

سنگهر sanghar, necklace. Si.

سوا sawá, except, without. P.

سواد sawád, sight, show.

سوارک sawárak, breakfast.

سواس sawás, Baloch sandals, made of the leaves of the dwarf palm.

سوال sawál, question. A.

سواه sawáh, morning. A. sabáh.

سوبهه sobh, victory. A.

سود súd, interest. P.

سور sor, salt, brackish, saltpetre. P. shor.
sore*n*-áf, brackish water.

سودا saudá, bargain. P.

سوره súrah, hero, warrior. Si. Súrihu. Z. súra, strong.

سوز savz, green. P. sabz.

سوشغ sosha*gh*, v., p.p. so*kh*ta, to burn. P. so*kh*tan, soz.

سوغن sau*gh*an, oath.

sang*h*an-zíra*gh*, to take an oath.

سوف súf, apple. A.

سوك sawakk, light (in weight).

سول sol, the kanda or jhand tree. (*Prosopis spicigera.*)

سومر somar, Monday. Si.

سونارو sonáro, goldsmith. Si.

سوهان sauhán, file.

سوهنا sohná, beautiful. Panj.

سوهو sohav, guide, acquaintance.

سوو savav, account, reason. A. sabab.

savavá, on account of.

سويث swe*th*, white. P. safíd.

سهارل sahàral, skilful.

سهاگ suhág, young unweaned camel up to six months old (f.)

سهبت suhbat, society. A.

سهاري sihárí, an awl. Si. síráí.

سهث sah*th*, jewels.

سهر suhr, red. P. sur*kh*. Pashto súr.

سهر sihr, magic. P.

sihr-khano*kh*, magician.

سهرا sahra, manifest, known, evident. A.

سهو suhv, morning. Ar. sub*h*.

suhv-astár, morning star.

سهيل suhel, autumn. The month Assú or Ásoj. A. (Sept. or Oct.)

سي sí, thirty. P.

سي sai, three. P. sih.

sai-bará, thrice.

sai-kona, triangle.

sai-gíst, threescore.

سياد syád, relation.

سيال syál, relation, guest, enemy, equal. (Pashto siál, equal.)

سيالداري syáldárí, relationship.

سياه syáh, black. P.

syáh-áf, } perennial stream of water.
syáh-jo, }

syáh-már, snake.

syáh-gwar, "black breast." The black partridge.

سياهي syáhí, ink.

سيبک sebak, wholesome.

سيث síth, profit, advantage. P. súd.

سير ser, full, satisfied.

seráf, satisfied. P. seráb.

سير sír, marriage.

sír-khanagh, to marry.

sír-bíagh, to be married.

sír-wájh, marriageable.

سيرب serab, shaving.

سيرمغ sírmugh, collyrium for the eyes. P. surma.

سيستان sístán, custom.

سيسي sesí, the chakor, also the sísí or *Ammo Perdix Bouhami.*

سيشن síshin, needle. P. sozan.

سيک saiak, one-third.

سيکن síkun, } porcupine.
سيخن síkhun, }

síkun-tír, porcupine-quill.

سيلهي selhí, necklace of shells worn by mares, camels, oxen, &c. Si.

سيم sím, boundary.

سيماندر símándar, neighbour.

سيمون símsún. See sesí.

سيمي saimí, third.

سيند sínd, hissing. (Si. sindh, whistling.)

sindá khanagh, to hiss.

سينز senz, whistling.

senzár janagh, to whistle.

سينزده senzdah, thirteen. P.

سينغ senagh, breast. P. sína.

سیوال sewál, s. rubbish left by a flood.

سیه síh, spit. P. sí*kh*.

tufak-síh, ramrod.

سیها síhá, lead. Si.

سیہنغ sehna*gh*, v. to bear, endure. Si. sahnu.

سیئغ sía*gh*, v., p.p. sí*th*a, to swell. P. ámá-sídan.

ش Sh.

شا shá. See shawá, you. P.

شاثلو shá*th*lo, dove.

شاخ shá*kh*, branch. P.

شاذي shá*dh*í, rejoicing, merry-making. P. shádí.

شار shár, (Ar. شعر), poem.

شاغ shá*gh*, a small tree (*Grewia Vestita*).

شاغا shá*gh*á, guitar or banjo. See dambíro.

شال shál, blanket. P.

شام shám, the evening meal. P.

شان shán, power, powerful, honourable. Ar.

شان 'shán, for ashán, from that.

'shán-go, thence.

'shán-phalawá, from that direction.

شاند shánd, sign.

شانزده shá*n*zdah, sixteen. P.

شانغ shána*gh*, backbone, nape of neck. P. shána.

شانکهه shánkh, stony ground at foot of hills.

شاه sháh, horn.

شاه sháh, king. P.

sháh-murdán, forefinger.

شاهکپتر sháhkaptar. See shafkástir.

شاهد sháhid, witness. Ar.

شاهدي sháhidí, evidence.

شاهي sháhí, a 2-anna piece. P.

شاير sháir, (Ar. شاعر), poet.

شبچراغ shabchirá*gh*, firefly. P.

شدت shiddat, disputing, argument. Ar.

شدو shaddo, a turban (poet). Si. shado.

شذغ shu*dhagh*, v., p.p. shustha, to hunger.

شذغ shu*dhagh*, v., p.p. shustha, to wash, intr.

شذي shu*dhí*, adj. hungry.

شر sharr, good, fine, beautiful.

شرت shart, gambling. A.

شردو shurdo, a small species of Dianthus found on the Sulaiman Range.

شرا shará, a law-case. A.

شرم sharm, shame. P.

شرو shurú, beginning. A.

شریک sharík, partner. A.

شست shist, sight of a gun. P.

شستغ shasta*gh*, v. p.p. shastátha, to send. Cf. P. firistádan.

شش shash, six. P.

ششمي shashumí, sixth.

شار shár, poem. A.

شغر sha*gh*ar, sharp, harsh (in speech).

شغان sha*ghá*n, scorn, mockery.

شغين shi*ghí*n, upside down, topsy-turvy.

shi*ghí*n-bía*gh*, to be upset.

شف shaf night. P. shab.

shaf-chirá*gh*, firefly.

shaf-kástir, a plant. *Sophora Griffithii.*

shaf-khor, nightblind.

شفانکھ shafánkh, shepherd, goatherd. P. shabán.

شفک shafak, s. iron peg on which a mill stone revolves.

شک shakk, doubt. A.

شکار shikár, hunting, sport. P.

شکاري shikárí, hunter.

شکر shukr, thanks. A.

شکھل shakhal, tamarisk sugar. (The manna produced in the hot weather on *Tamarix articulata* and *Tamarix gallica*). P. shakar.

شکھل shakhal, adj. sweet, fair.

شلوار shalwár, } the loose trowsers worn by Balochis.
شلور shalwar, }

gwá*th*-shalwar, puffed up, proud.

شم sham, boundary, water-parting.

شمب shamb, branch.

شمشغ shamusha*gh*, } p.p. shamushta, to forget. Cf. P. faráoshídan.
شموشغ shamúsha*gh*, }

شمول shamol, water-parting.

شنز shinz, the camel-thorn. (*Alhagi Mauroram.*) Cf. Pashto, zoz.

شنکھ shanikh, kid (f.)

شوکش shav-kash. For shaf-kash, the night-expeller, *i. e.* Venus, the morning star.

شوا shawá, } you. P. shumá.
شا sh'á, }

شوانکھ shawánkh. See shafánkh, shepherd.

شوذغ sho*dh*a*gh*, p.p. shustha, to wash. P. shustan.
ján-sho*dh*a*gh*, to bathe.

شورغ shora*gh*, saltpetre. P. shora.

شوشکغ shawashka*gh*, v., p.p. shawa*kh*tha, to sell. (Cf. P. faro*kh*tan).

شوکغ shúka*gh*, to smell.

شوم shúm, miser, avaricious. Ar.

شوھازکھنغ shúház-khana*gh*, to like, prefer.

شھر shahr, town, village. P.

شھور shahúr, good manners. Ar.

شي sh'í. Contraction for ash-í, from this.
sh-í phalawá, from this direction.

شيدي shídí, a negro. Ar.

شيذ she*dh*, hence, from here. (For ash-e*dh*.)

شیذپھذا shed*h*-phad*há*, henceforward.

شیذا shed*há*, hence.

شیخن shí*kh*an, s. cloth in which the flour from the mill is collected.

شیر shír, milk. P.

shír-wár, suckling, unweaned.

shír-deo*kh*, milch.

shír-dosho*kh*, milker.

shír-dán, bladder.

شیر sher, under, from under. (P. zer.)

sher-phalavá, from the underside.

sher-gwá*th*, leeward.

sher-thara*gh*, to be crushed beneath.

شیزرک shezirk, a low furze-like shrub, (*Caragana* sp.)

شیف shef, slope. P. shíb, nishíb.

áf-shef, watershed, slope of a drainage basin.

شیفغ shefa*gh*, pin or rod for applying collyrium to the eyes.

غ Gh.

غرق *gh*arra*gh*, to snore.

غریب *gh*aríb, poor, inoffensive. A.

غلت *gh*alat, mistake, false statement. A.

غلام *gh*ulám, a slave. A.

غم *gh*am, grief, sorrow. A.

غمناک *gh*amnák, sorrowful. A. P.

غمي *gh*amí, mourning. A.

ف F.

فال fál, an omen. Ar.

فایده fáida, advantage, profit. P.

فرشتغ firishta*gh*, angel. See phirishta*gh*. P.

فرق fark, difference. Ar.

فصل fasl, harvest. Ar.

فلاسي falásí, carpet, Ar.
فلانه fuláua, certain, such a one. Ar.

ك K.

كابل kábil, able. A.
كاتر kátar, dagger.
كار kár, work, business. P.
كارچ kárch, } knife. P. kárad.
كارچه kárcha, }
كاري kárí, basket. See khárí.
كاريز kárez, underground aqueduct.
كاريگر kárígar, ox.
كازي kází, the Qáẕí. A.
كاسه kása, a measure of corn, one-sixth of a harwár. Contains about 6 sers, 9 chitáks Indian weight.
كاشد káshid, messenger. A.
كاغذ kág*hadh*, letter. P.
كافر káfir, unbeliever. A.
كاک kák, Baloch bread baked round a heated stone.
كالرا kálrá, flea. Si. kárịro.
كامباني kámbání, sling.
كان kán, mine. P.
كانديري kánderí, thistle. Si. káṇḍerí.
كانوني ká*n*wní, cormorant.
كاوش káosh, the month of Ásoj.
كاهي káhí, ditch. See kháhí.
كبر kabr, tomb. A.
كبول kabúl, acceptance, agreement. A.
كبه kubba, a domed building.
كپتغ kapta*gh*, v. to attack.
كپنيغ kapaina*gh*, to expend.

کٹ kut, blunt.
کت kut, lap.
کتاکھنغ kutákhanagh, to adopt.
کتار katár, string of camels. A.
کتب kutb, the North Pole.
kutb-astár, the polestar.
کتري katre, a little while. A. qadr.
کتغ kuttigh, thorn.
کتنوخ kuttanokh, thorny bushes. Two or three species of *Caragana*.
کتھ kath, spinning. Si.
کتھان kithán, which? what?
کتي kutti, death.
کٹرغ kuṭragh, to gnaw.
کٹغ kaṭagh, to dig, conquer, overcome.
کٹغ kuṭagh, to thrash. Si. kuṭanu.
کٹکر kaṭakar, sand-grouse. Si. kaṭangar.
کثان kithán. See kithán.
کجغ kajagh, v., p.p. kajatha, to cover. Si. kajanu.
کجل kajal, coarse flood grass.
کچ کھنغ kach-khanagh, to measure. Si. kachh.
کچتوي kuchtoe, a plant.
کچہري kachehrí, an assembly, darbar. H.
کدال kudál, a mattock. Si. koḍari.
کده kadah, a cup. P.
کذام kudhám, s. nest.
کذين kadhen, when?
کر kur, a stable, Si. kuṛhi.
کرا karrá, ring, link of a chain. S. kaṛo.
کرپاس karpás, cotton. Skr. karpása.
کراکٹ karákuṭ, noise, rattling, clashing.
کرتا kurtá, long coat. Si. kurto.
کرتي kurtí, short coat. Si. kurtí.

كرثغ kar*thagh*, mongrel, of mixed breed.
كرشك kirishk, a slip, stumble.
كرشكغ kirishka*gh*, to slip, stumble. Si. khiskanu.
كركاوغ karkáva*gh*, a thorny plant.
كركني karkaní, a kind of grass.
كرم kirm, insect, worm. P.
كرمساكهه karmsákh, blackguard, a term of abuse.
كرويلي karvelí, the caper bush. (*Capparis spinosa.*) Si. kalavári.
See go*dhán*-din.
كري karrí, an earring. Si.
كري kirrí, a Baloch hut. Si. Pashto.
كريهه kireh, hire, wages. P. kiráya.
كڙ kiṛ, ashes. Si. kiri.
كزغ kiza*gh*, p.p. kishtha, to leave.
كس kas, any, any one. P. kas.
kase, some one.
har-kas, every one.
كس kus, vulva.
كساين kisái*n*, } little, small. P. kih, kihtar.
كسان kisán, }
كسانك kisának, very small.
كسهه kissa, story. A.
كشك kashk, kaurí.
كشك kshik, dog (m.)
كشكول kashkol, faqír's begging dish.
كل kil, a wart.
كل kull, all, the whole. A.
kullá-phajyá, altogether.
كل kal, knowledge, skill. Si.
كلات kilát. (Ar. قلعة), a fort.
كلاي kaláí, tin. P.
كلتري kaltrí, a saw.
كلدار kaldár, of European manufacture, as a gun, a rupee.

کلشک kulishk, a kind of grass.

کلغ kulla*gh*, to cough. See khulla*gh*.

کلف kulaf, lock. P. kufl.

کلو kulo, a small earthen pot. See khulo.

کله kulla, cap.

کله kulla, a warning.

کم kam, little, few. P. (Also kham.)

کم‌بخت kamba*kh*t, unlucky. P.

کمب kumb, tank, pool, rock hollow containing water.

کمبر kambar, variegated, stained. See khambar-kambar khana*gh*, to write.

کمبیغ kumbí*gh*, s. mushroom. S. khumbí.

کمینه kamína, mean, low. P.

کنت kunt, blunt.

کنتغ kunta*gh*, thorn.

کنجري kanjarí, prostitute. Si.

کنجي kunjí, key. Si.

کنچثه kunchi*th*a, a plant.

کنچیث kunchí*th*, sesamum. See kwenchi*gh*. P. kunjid.

کند kund, near. See khund.

کندغ kanda*gh*, a mountain pass. See khanda*gh*.

کندي kandí, necklace.

کندي kundí, a hook. Si.

کندغ kinda*gh*, p.p. kinda*th*a, to spread out. Si. khinḍanu.

کنر kunar, the ber-tree, jujube-tree. P.

dig-kunar, *Zizyphus jujuba*.

khokar-kunar, *Z. nummularia*.

thola*gh*-kunar, *Z. oxyphylla*.

کني kany, a virgin. Si. kanyá.

کواٹ kawáṭ, a young male camel up to 3 years. Si.

کوان kawán, bow. Share of spoil taken in a raid. P. kamán.

کوانٹغ kwánṭa*gh*, to stoop.

کوتله kotila, young camel from 6 months to 1 year old.

کوچ kúch, s. pommel of saddle.

کودي kodí, metal cup for drinking.

کوڈال koḍál, mattock. See kuḍál.

کور kor. See khor.

کور kaur, the phaláhí-tree *(Acacia modesta)*.

کورو koro, whip. H. korí.

کورکي korkí, trap, snare. Si.

کوش kaush, Baloch shoes. P. kafsh. Pashto, kośha.

کوک kavg, the chakor. P. kabk.

کولمیر kolmír, an aromatic plant; (*Grantea*, sp.) Si.

کونتر kontar, a bush. (*Grewia*, sp. ?).

کونتر kontar, a pigeon. P. kabútar.

کونر konar, the fruit of the dwarf palm *(Chamærops ritchieana)*.

کوه koh, mountain; stone. P.

koh-gurá*gh*, raven.

کوهي kohí, the female már*kh*or.

کوینچغ kwenchi*gh*, }
کنچغ kunchi*gh*, } til *(Sesamum indicum)*. P. kunjid.

کها kahá, cause, reason.

کهاڈي kháḍí, chin. Si.

کهاري khárí, a basket. Si.

کهاریغر khárí*gh*ar, an ox.

کهال khál, a species of salsola. Also the sajjí or barilla manufactured from it.

کهاهي kháhí, a ditch. Si.

کهپتغ khapta*gh*, to attack.

کهتري khatrí, a washerman. Si.

کهٹ khaṭ, }
کهٹره khaṭra, } bedstead, charpoy. Si.

khaṭ-phá*dh*a*gh*, the four stars forming the body of Ursa Major.

کهجي khají, the date palm *(Phœnix dactylifera)*. Si.

کھڈ khaḍ, hole, pit. Si.

کھر khar, ass (f.). P. *kh*ar.

کہر kahar, auger, curse. Ar.

کھر khar, deaf. P. kar.

کھرپھز kharphaz, a mattock.

کھرد khard, separate.

khard-bía*gh*, to be separated.

کھردغ khurda*gh*, to be scattered.

کھردي kharde, some. (Cf. A. P. qadre).

کھرغ khura*gh*, a colt.

کھرغا khar*ghá*, above.

کھرگ kharag, the ák-bush, (*Calatropis procera*).

کھرگز khargaz, the vulture. Pashto, gargas.

کھرگوشک khargoshk, the hare. P. *kh*argosh.

کھروبیدُغ kharo-bía*gh*, to stand up. Si. B.

کھري khurí, heel, hoof. Si. khuṛí.

کھڑ khuṛ, stable.

کھس khas. See kas. P.

کھشالا khishálá, difficulty, trouble.

کھشار khishár, cultivation, crops.

کھشار khushár, slaughter.

کھشغ khasha*gh*, v., p.p. khashtha, to draw, turn out, discharge, blow (of the wind). P. kashtan.

phost-khasha*gh*, to flay.

phor-khasha*gh*, to smoke a pipe.

hon-khasha*gh*, to bleed, tr.

líkh-khasha*gh*, to draw a line.

gwá*th*-khasha*ghen*, the wind is blowing.

کھشغ khisha*gh*, v., p.p. khishtha, to cultivate. P. khishtan.

کھشغ khusha*gh*, v., p.p. khushtha, to kill. P. kushtan.

کھفغ khafa*gh*, v., p.p. khaptha, to fall, lie down. To begin (qualifying another verb in the gerund).

khana*ghá* khafa*gh*, to begin to do.

er-khafa*gh*, to descend, come down, alight.

dar-khafa*gh*, to come out, issue.

daryá dar-khaptha, the river has risen in flood.

کہکہر khakhar, wasp. (Sindhi. See gwamz).

khakhar-mánáro, wasp's nest.

کہل khil, peg or axle on which a millstone revolves.

کہلغ khulla*gh*, to cough.

کہلگر khalgar, stony ground ; large stones.

کہلو khulo, an earthen pot or *loṭa*.

کہلي khalí, a small water skin (kid's skin) carried on journeys. (Si. khaliṛí, skin).

کہلير khaler, the *Capparis aphylla*.

کہليرو khalero, wild asparagus.

کہم kham, little, less. P. kam.

کہمب khumb, pool in a stream. See kumb.

کہمبر khambar, variegated, striped, spotted, piebald, stained, (of animals).

کہناوه khanáwa, a sword, (poet.). Si. khano.

کہند khund, adv. near. S. A piece of ground enclosed by a bend in a torrent bed.

کہندغ khanda*gh*, s. a pass over a crest or ridge.

کہندغ khandagh, v., p.p. khandi*th*a, to laugh. P. *kh*andídan.

کہنغ khanagh, v., p.p. khu*th*a, to do. P. kardan, kun. To be able, can (qualifying a preceding verb in the past participle) ; *e. g.*, khu*th*a khanán, I can do.

er-khana*gh*, to lay down, place.

el-khana*gh*, to imprison.

áwár-khana*gh*, to mix.

bahr-khana*gh*, to divide.

phol-khana*gh*, to ask, enquire.

phur-khana*gh*, to fill.

jalo-khana*gh*, to attack.

kach-khana*gh*, to measure.

gur-khana*gh*, to run away.

much-khana*gh*, to collect.

كهنغ kahna*gh*, old clothes, rags.

كهنوخ khano*kh*. Verbal noun from khana*gh*, doer.

كهنه kahna and kuhna, old. P.

كهني kahne, s. pigeon.

كهني kuhne, s. hip.

كهوپر khopar, skull. Si. kopirí.

كهوپرا khoprá. The *Withiana coagulans* used for curdling milk.

كهوخر kho*kh*ar, a kind of wild turnips (*Brassica*, sp.)

كهودغ khúda*gh*, a tripod for cooking.

كهور khaur, a large hill torrent. (Cf. Pashto *kh*war.)

كهور khor, blind. P.

كهوري khorí, pursuit.

كهوسا khosá, fever. Panj.

كهوفغ khofa*gh*, shoulder.

khofa*gh* juzaina*gh*, to shrug the shoulders.

كهوفغا khofa*gh*á, the shoulder muscles.

كهولو khaulú, a fawn.

كهونتر khontar, a bush, (*Carissa diffusa*).

كهونجر khawinjar, a partridge.

كهونڈ khonḍ, the knee.

khonḍ bhoraina*gh*, to kneel.

كهي khaí, } who ?

كهئيغين khaí*gh*en, } whose ?

كهير khair, ox.

كهير kahír, the kanda or jhand tree, *Prosopis spicigera*. See also Sol.

كهير kher, the penis. P. kír.

كهيزان khaizá*n*, perhaps, may be.

كهيسغ khísa*gh*, pouch, pocket. P. kísa.

كهين khín, the anus.

khíná-phur-bio*kh*, a breechloader.

کہیندر khíndar, naked.
کہینو khenú, a ball. Si. kheno.
کیتغ kíta*gh*, a water-melon.
کیغو kai*gh*o, itch, mange. Si kháji.
کیلار kílár, unripe fruit of *Chamærops ritchieana*.
کینگ kínag, envy, grudge. P. kína.
کیوا kíwá, in exchange.

گ G.

گادي gádí, pad, cushion. Si.
گار gár, lost, destroyed.
gár-bía*gh*, to be lost.
gár-khana*gh*, to lose, make away with.
گار gár. See gál, speech. Si.
گارا gárá, quarrel.
گاغ gá*gh*, v., p.p gá*th*a, coire.
گال gál, speech. Si. gálhu.
گالور gálwar, conversation, matter of discourse.
گالي gálí, a visit.
گالي gálí, bedding.
گام gám, a pace.
gámá juza*gh*, to walk (of a horse).
گپ gap, quicksand, quagmire. Si.
گپہل gaphall, a piece, bit. Si. gapalu.
گتني guttaní, retreating.
گتہا githá, cheek.
گٹ gaṭ, chasm, precipice.
گٹغ guṭṭi*gh*, the kidney.
گٹور gaṭúr. See ghatúr.
گٹہہ guṭh, the throat.
گڈہي guṭhí, bridle.
گڈي gaṭṭí, wooden handcuffs. Si.
گج gaj, a wooden arrow.

گچ guch, the colocynth gourd, bitter apple. *Cucumis Colocynthis.*

گدکهه gadikh, kernel.

گدوبر gadobar, maize.

گدي gudí, a toy-kite.

گڈ gaḍ, female uriál. (See guránḍ). (Cf. Pashto, gaḍ ram).

گڈا guḍá, then, again, and.

گڈغ guḍa*gh*, to chop, to kill animals, to butcher. Si. guḍanu.

گڈي gaḍí, the middle finger.

گذ gu*dh*, cloth.

گر gar, a pimple, boil.

گر gur, s. kauṛí.

گر gur, running.

گرکهنغ gur-khana*gh*, to run away. Cf. Pehl. giríkht, fled.

گڑا gaṛrá, piebald, skewbald (of a horse).

گراذغ grá*dh*a*gh*, v., p.p. grástha, to boil.

گرارتهه girárth, a span (with the thumb and 3rd finger).

گراغ gurá*gh*, crow.

koh-gurá*gh*, raven.

گران girán, heavy, dear. P.

گرانڈ guránḍ, a ram. The male uriál. (*Ovis cycloceros*).

گراني giráni, weight, dearth. P.

گرانز grá*n*z, nostril.

گربرا gurburá, in a whisper. Si. guṛbuṛí.

گرپهغ gurphu*gh*, small-pox.

گرپهيل garphíl, a whirling cloud of dust or "devil."

گرجغ girja*gh*, to catch, seize, p.p. girjí*th*a.

گردغ garda*gh*, v., p.p. gartha, to return. P. gardídan.

گردن gardan, neck. P.

گردينغ gardaina*gh*. Causal of garda*gh*.

گرذغ gra*dh*a*gh*, v., p.p. grastha, to cook.

گرغ gira*gh*, v., p.p. gipta, imp. gír. P. giriftan, gír, to take, accept, seize, lay hold of.

bál-gira*gh*, to fly.

bo-gira*gh*, to smell.
hál-gira*gh*, to hear news.
zahr-gira*gh*, to be angry.
sar-gira*gh*, to set out.

گرغ garra*gh*, to roar or bellow.
گرکغ gurka*gh*, to growl. Si. guranu.
گرکهه gurkh, wolf. P. gurg.

gurkh, the Wolf, *i. e.*, the last star in the tail of *Ursa major*. See under Guránḍ.

گرم garm, hot, warm. P.
گرنچ granch, a knot.
گرند garand, thunder.
گراند guránḍ, (1) ram; (2) the male urial *(Ovis cycloceros)*.

Guránḍ, the Ram, *i. e.*, the first star of the three forming the tail of *Ursa major*. This is supposed to be pursued by the second, the Dog, which in its turn is pursued by the last star, the Wolf.

Guránḍ-drikh, the Milky Way (lit. the Ram's leap). This refers to the legend of the Ram brought from heaven to take the place of Ismáíl when Abraham was about to sacrifice him. The Milky Way is supposed to be the Ram's track.

گرندغ garanda*gh*, v., p.p. garanda*th*a, to thunder.
گروخ giro*kh*, s. lightning.
گروخ giro*kh*. Verbal noun from gira*gh*, a taker, creditor.
گروه giroh, s. fife, pipe.
گري garí, speech, song.
گري garí, bald.
گڑري gaṛrí, piebald, skewbald (of a mare).
گريغ gire*gh*, v., p.p. girentha, to weep. P. girgán.
گريه gríh, voice, sound.

zor-gríhá, in a loud voice.

گڑ gaṛ, a precipice, sudden descent, chasm. Pashto, gaṛang.

گز gaz, tamarisk. Especially *Tamarix gallica.*

gíth-gaz, *Tamarix articulata.* P.

گز gaz, a yard.

گزر guzar, makeshift.

گزران guzrán, maintenance.

گزرین gazaren, ought, is necessary.

گزغ guza*gh*, v., p.p. gwastha, to pass. P. guzishtan.

guza*gh*-rava*gh*, to pass by.

گزیر gazír, miser.

گسر gisar, mistake, forgetting. Si. bisiranu.

gisar-bía*gh*, to forget.

گسور gasúr, s. anger.

گشت gasht, coarse long grass on the hill side, not eaten by cattle.

گشغ gusha*gh*, v., p.p. gushtha and gwashtha, to speak, say, tell, sing, recite. (Skr. vach).

گشوخ gusho*kh*, singer, reciter.

گشیدغ gishaina*gh*, v., p.p. gishaintha, to choose. P. gizídan.

گغ gu*gh*, owl. P. buh.

گفتار guftár, speech, song. P.

گفغ gufa*gh*. See گوفغ gwafa*gh*, to weave.

گل gal, cheek. Si. galu.

گل gal, a number, quantity. Used in composition to form nouns of quantity as jan-gal, a band of women.

گل gil, clay, earth. P.

گل gul, a flower. P.

گلاغ galá*gh*, p.p. galái*th*a, to praise.

گلالکهه gulálakh, long curls worn by Balochis.

گلپهان galphán, a groom, syce.

گلثه gala*th*a, rotten. Hindi, galá.

گلر gullar, dog's pups. Si. guliru.

گلغ gala*gh*, a band of mares, or of horsemen.

galagh-tháshí, horse-racing.

گلگل gulgul, water with which the mouth is rinsed after eating.

گلو galo, door.

گله galla, a káfila, caravan. Si.

گلي galí, a street. Si.

گليم galím, a rug or blanket. P.

گناس gunás, (rare) } fault, sin. P. gunáh.
گناه gunáh, (common) }

گنج gunj, crease, wrinkle. Si. gunyu. Pashto gunjah.

گنجي ganjí, a measure of corn.

گند gand, s. a branch water-course.

گند gand, s. filth, manure. P.

gand-bo, stink.

گند gund, testicles.

gundí, an entire horse.

گنداخو gandá*kh*o, Indian rue (*Peganum harmala*).

گندرف gandraf, sulphur. Si.

گندغganda*gh*, bad.

گندغ ganda*gh*, v., p.p. ganda*th*a, to join.

گندغ ginda*gh*, v., p.p. ديثه dí*th*a, imp. gind, to see. P. bín, dídan.

گندل gandal, s. felt, namda.

گنديل gandíl, a short fodder grass in the lower Sulaimáns and plains. Si.

گنديم gandím, wheat. (P. gandum.)

گنڐ ganḍ, Adam's apple.

گنوخ ganno*kh*, fool, idiot.

asulá-ganno*kh*, a born idiot.

گو go, prep. with. P. bá.

گو go, s. race, prize.

go-bar, a race-winner.

گواث gwá*th*, air, wind. P. bád.

gwá*th*-má, climate.

er-gwá*th*á, on the leeside.

gwá*th*-shalwar, puffed up.

گواڈغ gwá*th*a*gh*, a gelding.

گواڈو gwá*th*o, windy.

gwá*th*en hálwar khana*gh*, to talk big.

گورش gwárish, rain. P. bárish.

گواز gwáz, bark of a tree.

گواش gwásh, ground at the foot of a hill.

گوافغ gwáfa*gh*, v., p.p. gwáptha, to call together, summon. (Cf. P. guftan.)

گواغا gwá*gh*á, immediately.

گوالغ gwála*gh*, packsaddle for oxen, bags.

ganda-gwála*gh*, (lit. spoil-bags), the small red ant. Also the name of a Baloch sub-tribe.

گوامیش gwámesh, buffalo. P. gáv-mesh.

گوامیش gwámísh, a small plant used in washing.

گوان guwán, doubt, hesitation. P. gumán.

گوانزغ gwá*n*za*gh*, a swinging cradle.

گوانکهه gwá*n*kh, voice, sound. P. báng.

gwá*n*kh-jana*gh*, gwán'-jana*gh*, } to call out.

گوبر go-bar, a horse that has won a race.

گوت got, bridegroom. Panj.

گوج goj, a large lizard, "go-sámp." Si.

گوچ gwach, a buffalo-calf. Si. vachhi. Skr. vatsa.

گوخ go*kh*, an ox, cow. P. gáv.

گوخ gau*kh*, nape of the neck.

گوخراند go*kh*ránd, dung-beetle.

گوخو go*kh*o, a span with the thumb and forefinger. Si. goṇkú.

گودر godur, a plant.

گودي godí, mistress, lady.

گوذ go*dh*, menstruation.

گوزان gwa*dh*án or go*dh*án, udder.

gwa*dhán*-din, the caper-plant. *Capparis spinosa.* (lit. udder-tearer).

گوذر go*dh*ar, wasp's nest.

گور gwar, adv. near. P. bar.

gwará, nearly.

گور gor, wild ass. P.

gor-dil, *Daphne mucronata* (so called from its red berries).

گور gor, } tomb.
گورستان goristan, }

گور gwar, woman's breast. P. bar.

gwar-sar, nipple.

gwará*n* dír khanu*gh*, to wean.

gwar-ambází, embracing.

گورانڈ goránḍ, a ram, male uriál.

گوربند gwarband, path leading round the foot of a hill.

گور پهر gwarpahar, flock of lambs.

گورغ gwara*gh*, v., p.p. gwartha, fut. 3rd pers. sing. gwárí, to rain. P. báridan.

گورکهه gwara*kh*, a lamb.

گورکها gorkhá, a kind of coarse grass called in Sind and the S. Panjáb sin or sain, good for fodder.

گورم goram, a herd of cattle. (P. gáv, rama.) (Si. goramu.)

گوڑ gúṛ, gur or coarse molasses.

گوزغ gwaza*gh*. See گزغ guza*gh*, to pass. P. guzashtan.

گوژد gozhd, flesh, meat. P. gosht.

گوس gwas, enough. P. bas.

گوسکري goskarí, crystal, felspar; fossils in rock.

گوش gosh, ear. P.

gosh-dea*gh*, to listen, attend.

گوشا goshá, s. the pan of a matchlock.

گوشغ gwasha*gh*. See گشغ gusha*gh*, to say.

گوغرا go*gh*rá, s. a snore. Go*gh*rá jana*gh*, to snore.

گوفغ gwafa*gh*, v., p.p. gwaptha, to weave. (P. báftan.)

گوکرد gokurd, sulphur. P.

گوماڈ gomá*dh*, a kind of grass, the seed of which is eaten in times of scarcity, called in Sindh and the Deraját, gam. *Panicum antidotale.*

nar-gomá*dh*, a kind of grass with star-shaped flowers, found in the Upper Sulaimáns.

گومز gwamz, a wasp.

گون gon, with, together with.

gon-dea*gh*, to overtake.

gon-khafa*gh*, to meet.

گون gwan or gon, the wild pistachio. *Pistacia khinjuk.*

گوند gwand, short.

گونداڈ gwandá*dh*, shortness.

گوندو gwando, an alligator.

گوندوش gondosh, s. a large needle.

گونگ gúng, dumb. Si.

گونگرو gúngrú, turnip. See zang. Si.

گوہ goh, a large lizard. Si.

گوھار gohár, sister. P. khwáhar.

گوھر gwahar, cold.

گویل goil, s. breakfast-time.

گہٹ ghaṭ, inaccessible place, precipice.

گہٹّغ ghaṭṭa*gh*, v. to smother.

گہٹّور ghaṭúr, a lamb or young sheep suitable for eating. (Cf. Si. ghaṭo, ram).

گہر guhar, adj. See گوم gwahar.

گہریاي ghuriáí, s. a stranger.

گہڑي ghaṛí, hour. Si.

گہل ghal, a band, a raiding party, a raid. Si. ghali.

گہن gahn, a pledge. Si. gahno.

گہوڑو ghoṛo. A band of horsemen. (Si. ghoṛo, horse.)

گيانچ giánch, a small bird found in sandy parts of the country, called Malála in the Deraját.

گيتره getra, a kind of melon.

گيث geth, the willow, *Salia acmophylla*. P. bed.

گيثشک gethishk, the Sinetta or Bog-myrtle. *Dodonæa viscosa.*

گيث‌گر gith-gaz, a kind of Tamarisk. *T. articulata.*

گيذمهسک gídh-mahisk, house-fly.

گير gír. Imp. of giragh, take.

گير gír, s. memory.

gír-áragh, to remember.

girár deagh, to remind.

گيرا gírá, dove. Si. gero. (See sháthlo.)

گيژغ gezhagh, v., p.p. gikhta, to bring forth dead offspring.

گيست gíst, twenty, sai-gíst, 60, chyár-gíst, 80. P. bíst.

گيستمي gístumí, twentieth.

گيش gísh, s. a female kid.

گيشتر gíshtar, a shrub, *Periploca aphylla*.

گيستر geshtar, many, more. P. beshtar.

گيشن geshin, a sieve.

گيکار gíkár, belch.

گيلر gelar, a squirrel. Hindi galeṛí.

گين gín, life, breath.

do-gín, pregnant.

گيها gehá, great, good.

گييشغ gíeshagh, v., p.p. gíeshtha, to pick out, to pay.

ل L.

لاپهر láphur, (láf-phur), pot-bellied, pregnant.

لاڈ láḍ, sport, play. Si. láḍu.

láḍá khanagh, to play.

لار lár, s. crookedness.

لاغ lágh, a male donkey.

لاغر lághar, thin, lean. P.

لاف láf, belly, stomach.

láf-band, belt.

láf-dor, bellyache.

láf-ser, bellyful.

لاکغ lákagh, to bark.

لال lál, ruby. P.

لانو lánav, lana, *(Salsola sueda)*. Si. láno.

لاندو lándav, adj. fat.

لانک lánk, a waistcloth, dhoti. Si. láng.

لاورا láwará, young of animals.

لاینغ láinagh, v., p.p. láitha, to touch, apply. Si. láinu.

لب lab, the priming of a gun. Si. labu.

lab-chaṭagh, to flash in the pan.

لبز labz, promise.

لبھہ labh, obtaining, getting. Si.

لتارغ latáragh, to rub off, dismiss, get rid of. Si. latáṛanu.

لتھہ lath, stick, rod, flail. Si. laṭhi.

لٹھہ laṭh, embankment. Panj.

لٹھنا laṭhná, bag for drugs.

لج laj, shame. Si.

لچ luch, wretch, profligate. Si. luchu.

لڈ liḍ, horse-dung. Si.

لذغ ladagh, v. to run away.

لڈغ luḍagh, to move. See lodagh. Si. laṛanu.

لڈغ laḍagh, p.p. laḍatha, to lade beasts of burden, to march, start. Si. laḍanu.

لذ ladh, jungle.

لذغ ladhagh, kick. P. laghat.

ladhagh janagh, to kick.

لر lar, a branch of a tree.

لر lar, a sword.

لرزغ larzagh, to tremble. P.

p.p. larzitha.

لڑکغ laṛkagh, to hang (intr.). Si. laṭkanu.

لڑکینغ laṛkainagh, to hang (tr.).

لس las, all, the whole.

لشکر lashkar, army. P.

لغام la*gh*ám, horse's bit. P. lagám.

لغذ la*ghadh*, kick. See لذغ la*dhagh*.

لغر la*gh*ar, áf-la*gh*ar, a rapid or water-fall.

لغشغ la*gh*usha*gh*, v., p.p. la*gh*ushtha, to slip, slip out. (Ar. la*gh*z, slip).

لغور la*gh*or, adj. wretched, mean, cowardly, poor.
la*gh*ore*n* di*gh*ár, poor ground.
la*gh*ore*n* ḍaḍḍav, a wretched pony.

لک lak, a hundred thousand. P.

لکغ lika*gh*, to hide (intr.). Si. likanu.

لکوري lakaurí, butterfly.

لکهغ likha*gh*, to write. Si. likhanu.

لکينغ likaina*gh*, to hide, conceal. (Causal of lika*gh*.)

لله lalla, s. lisping.
lalla khana*gh*, to lisp.

لما lammá, south. Panj.

لمب lamb, a branch.

لمبي lambí, s. a kind of grass, *(Cenchrus eclimatus ?)*

لنج lanj, blood.

لنگ lang, adj. lame. P.

لنگ lang, s. a torrent.

لواشغ lawásha*gh*, v., p.p. lawáshtha, to drink.
hon-lawásh, bloodthirsty.
mar-lawásh, cannibal.

لوپ lop, s. branch of a valley; a small alluvial plain in the bend of a stream.

لوتهه loth, s. a bag.

لوٹغ loṭa*gh*, v., p.p. loṭ*th*a, to demand, to want.

لودغ loda*gh*, v., p.p. loda*th*a, to move, shake, (intr.). Si. loḍanu.

لوديغ lodaina*gh*, to shake (tr.). Causal of loda*gh*.

لور lúr, s. hot wind.

لور lawar, s. a stick.

لورهاف lúraháf, s. a stream which runs occasionally. Flood irrigation as distinguished from perennial stream irrigation.

لوري lorí, s. a minstrel.

لوغ lo*gh*, s. home, household; (met.) family, wife.
lo*gh*-wá*zh*á, goodman, master.
lo*gh*-bánukh, housewife, mistress.

لونڈري laundrí, s. the temples. Si. laundirí.

لوہ loh, s. hot wind. Si. lúh.

لوهيغ lohí*gh*, s. a small pond.

لہر lahar, s. a hill-torrent.

لہم lahm, adj. timid, bashful.

لہيف lihef, s. a blanket, quilt. P. liháf.

ليٹغ leṭa*gh*, v., p.p. leṭ*th*a, to lie, recline. Si. leṭanu.

ليڑو leṛo, s. a male camel (full-grown).

ليکھہ líkh, s. a line. Si. lík.
líkh khasha*gh*, to draw a line.

ليکھغ lekha*gh*, v., p.p. lekh*th*a, to count, reckon. Si. lekhanu.

ليکھو lekho, s. account, reckoning. Si.

ليلها lílhá, a bush, *Daphne mucronata*. (See phífal, gordil).

ليمو límú, s. lemon. A.

ليو lev, s. play, sport. A. la'b. Pashto lobah.
lev khana*gh*, to play.

م M.

ما má, pro. we, plural of ma*u*.

ماتون mátún, s. stepmother.

ماث má*th*, s. mother. P. mádar. Pehl. máḍ.
má*th*-phi*th*, parents.

ماختہ má*kh*ta, adv. immediately.

ماذغ má*dh*a*gh*, adj. female. P. máda.

ماذن má*dh*in, s. mare. P. mádián.

مار már, s. snake. P.
syahmár, cobra.

már-val, a kind of creeper.

مارفتا márifatá, prep. by means of. A.

ماري márí, a house with an upper storey. Si. máṛí.

مازاث mázá*th*, s. a two-year-old camel. (Cf. Si. májádu.)

ماسي mási, s. maternal aunt. Si.

ماش másh, s. dál. P.

ماشغ másha*gh*, s. the hammer which holds the match of a match-lock. Si. másho.

ماكورا mákúrá, s. vermin. (Cf. Si. mákoṛo, black ant.)

مال mál, s. cattle. A.

مالدار máldár, cattle-owner. P.

ماليم málím, known, clear. A. málúm.

ماما mámá, maternal uncle. Si. mámo.

مان mán, prep. in, into.

مان آغ mán-á*gh*, to be applied, touch, reach (lagná).

مان ديئغ man-dea*gh*, to apply (lagáná).

مان رشغ mán-rasha*gh*, to attack.

مان روغ mán-rava*gh*, to enter.

مان كهنغ mán-khana*gh*, to put in.

مان گزارغ mán-guzára*gh*, to meet together.

مانغ mána*gh*, v., p.p. mantha, to tire, become weary. P. mán-dan.

ماه máh, s. a month; the moon. P.

ماه غما máh-*gh*umá, eclipse of the moon.

ماهغ máhi*gh*, an udder.

ماهكان máhkán, s. the moon.

mahkání shaf, a moonlight night.

ماهلو máhlo, early in the morning.

ماهي máhí, fish. P.

متبل matbal, meaning, selfishness. (Ar. matlab.)

متبلي matbalí, selfish.

متهه math, death.

متهغ matha*gh*, v. to shake (a churn). Si. mathanu.

مت maṭ, equal. Si. maṭu.

متّينغ maṭṭainagh, v. to exchange, barter. Si. maṭáinu.

مجال majál, power. Used as an expression of apology or repentance. A.

مجالس majális, society. (A. majlis.)

مچ much, assembled. (Si. muchu, a heap.)

much-khanagh, to assemble, bring together.

much-bíagh, to assemble, come together.

مچهه muchh, joint.

phádh-muchh, ankle.

dast-muchh, wrist.

مچي muchí, assembly.

مخته makhta. See mákhta, immediately.

مد mudd, season, time. (A. muddat.)

مدرک madrik, bead.

مڈي maḍí, goods and chattels. Si.

مذخ madhakh, locust. P. malakh.

مذغ madhagh, v., p.p. mastha, to freeze, curdle. P: mastan.

مر mar, man. P. mard.

mar-khushokh, murderer.

mar-khushí, murder.

mar-lawásh, } cannibal, man-eating.
mar-wár, }

مراد murád, aim, object. A.

مراي maráí, gums.

مرجان murján, pepper.

مرد mard, man. P.

مردان murdán, s. finger.

sháh-murdán, forefinger.

nyámaghí murdán, middle-finger.

مردانغ murdánagh, the fingers.

phádh-murdánagh, the toes.

مردم mardum, a man, human being. P.

مردین marde*n*, } human, belonging to man.
مردینه mardena, }

مرزي marzí, pleasure. A.

مرغ mur*gh*, bird. P.

مرغ mira*gh*, v., p.p. murtha. Imp. mír, to die. P. murdan.

مرکا marká, s. a deputation.

مرکهو markhav, a horse. P. markab.

مرگاوي margáví, curse.

مرواذر murvá*dh*ir or murwhá*dh*ir, pearl. P. marvaríd.

مرورغ marora*gh*, to twist. Si. maroṛanu.

مرویهي marvehí, see! behold! (an expression of astonishment).

مروشي maroshí, to-day. P. imroz.

مڑاند miṛánd, } fight, battle.
مڑاو miṛáo, }

مڑاي maṛái, however.

مڑغ miṛa*gh*, v., p. p. miṛa*th*a, to fight. (Cf. Si. miḍanu, to meet.)

مڑوخ miṛo*kh*, s. a fighter.

مزاگرغ mazágira*gh*, to taste. P.

مزار mazár, tiger, &c. Pashto mzarai.

mazár-trap, tiger's leap! The name of a game resembling draughts played on a board.

مزین maza*in*, } great, large. Zend. mazdáo. Skr. mahá. P. mih.
مزن mazan, }

مزل mizil, stage, march. P. manzil.

مژ muzh, mist after rain.

مژغ mizha*gh*, v., p.p. mishtha, to piss.

Cf. Pashto mítal. Imp. mízhah.

مژگ mazhg, brain. P. ma*gh*z.

مژگژ mizhguzh, a small plant found in the Sulaimán range.

مژگان mizhagán. See mishásh.

مس mas, ink. Si.

مستر mastar, large, greater. (Comp. of maza*in*.)

مستغ masta*gh*, curds. (From masta, p.p. of ma*dhagh*.)

مستي mustí, coarse sugar or molasses, guṛ. Si.

مسرا masará, in front.

مسک misk, s. musk. P. mushk.

مسک misk. See mahisk, fly.

مسيت masít, mosque. A. masjid.

مشاذا mushá*dhá*, s. show.

مشاش mishásh, eyelashes.

مشال mashál, torch. A.

مشت musht, s. fist. P.

مشت musht, s. hilt of a sword.

مشر mashar, celebrated. (A. mashhúr.)

مشغ misha*gh*, v., p.p. mishta, to suck. (Cf. Ar. mizz.)

مشغ musha*gh*, v., p.p. mushta, to rub. (Cf. A. muzz.)

مشک mashk, water-bag, mussuck. P.

مشک mushk. See múshk.

مکراز mikráz, scissors.

مکهيرنا makherná, fringe over horse's eyes. See ríband. B.

ملامت malámat, rebuke, punishment, curse. A.

ملايخ maláiḵh, angel. A.

ملندري malandrí, warrior. (Poet.)

مم mam, the black bear.

من ma*n*, I. P.

منا manná, forbidden. Ar. mana.

منا minná, } ease, security. (Poet.)
منيا minniyá, }

منان maná*n*, to me, me.

منت minnat, entreaties, supplication. A.

مند mind, daughter (among the Marris).

مند mund, spring of water.

مندري mundrí, ring. Si. munḍrí.

مندو mundo, altogether, entirely.

منديل mandíl, turban, lungí.

du-mandíl, a respectable man.

منصف munsif, just. A.

منغ mana*gh*, v., p.p. mani*th*a, to attend, mind. Si. mananu.

مني maní, my. See also maí*n*.

مواركي mavárkí, congratulations.

موتهه moth, star on the forehead of a horse.

موٹهه moth, moth. (Dál). (*Phaseolus Aconitifolius*) Si.

موچي mochí, a leather worker. Si.

موخو mo*kh*o, spider.

mo*kh*o-lo*gh*, spider's web.

مور mor, ant. P.

موربند morband, spotted.

موژغ mozha*gh*, a boot, legging. P. moza.

موسم mosim, season. A. mausim.

موشک múshk, rat, mouse. P. músh. Skr. múshika.
Pashto mazhak.

موشن moshin, butter.

موکل mokal, leave, permission to depart. A.

موکلينغ mokalaina*gh*, to take leave. Old Hindí mukkalná.

مولد molid, a female slave.

مومريز momrez, spur.

مومند momand, merciful.

مهه mah, I. See ma*n*.

مهروان mihrván, friendly, kind. P. mihrbán.

مهري muharí, foremost, in front. Si. muháṛo.

مهر mahar, corpse.

مهسک mahisk, fly. (Cf. P. magas).

bena*gh*-mahisk, bee.

ḇíng-mahisk, horse-fly (lit. dog-fly).

gí*dh*-mahisk, house-fly.

ásk-mahis*k*, blow-fly (lit. deer-fly).

مهل mahl, patience, leisure. A.

mahlá-dár, be patient.

مهلت muhlat, time, while, opportunity. A.

مهمان mihmán, guest. P.

مهماني mihmání, entertainment. P.

مهيرا mahairá, in welfare, all's well. Answer to the salutation biyá durr'shá*kh*ta*gh*ei.

ميار mayár, shame.

ميچ mech, hint, making signs. Si. mechh.
dast-mechdea*gh*, to beckon.

ميخمار me*kh*már, mallet. Si.

ميذ mí*dh*, goat's hair or beard.

ميذ me*dh*, a boatman.

ميرو mero, s. assembly.

ميزغ meza*gh*. See mizha*gh*.

ميسك mesk, a small plant, also a kind of soap made from it, used in cleaning jewellery.

ميش mesh, sheep. Especially dumbas.

ميغي mai*gh*í, pregnant.

ميكغ míka*gh*, to mew.

ميگر megar, flock of sheep.

ميل mel, meeting. Si.

مينتهغ mentha*gh*, wet.

مينر mainar, a kind of grass.

مينهو mí*n*hav, a tree. The wild horseradish tree, *Moringa Concanensis.*

ميور maivar, a bush, *(Grewia villosa ?)*.

ميوو mevo, a chief, leader.

ميوه meva, fruit. P.

ميهه meh, peg. P. me*kh*.

ميهر mehar, flock of sheep.

ميهي mehí, buffalo. Si.

مئين mai*n*, my. See maní.

ن N.

نا ná, not, (un —, in composition).
نابالغ ná-báli*gh*, minor.
ناپيد ná-paid, uncommon.
نادراه ná-duráh, ill.
ناسهي ná-sahí, unknown.
ناكاما ná-kámá, helpless, under compulsion.
نالايک ná-láik, unworthy.
ناوش ná-wash, unhappy.
ناچيكين náchíke*n*, a little.
ناخن ná*kh*un, nail. P.
ناخو ná*kh*o, uncle (paternal).
ناخوزاخت ná*kh*ozá*kh*t, cousin. (Paternal uncle's son.)
نارغ nára*gh*, v., p.p. nári*th*a, to groan.
ناز náz, s. a horn (to blow).
ناز náz, pleasant, pretty. P.
نازبو názbo, sweet scent. P.
نازک názuk, delicate, tender. P.
ناش násh, snuff. Si. nás.
نافغ náfa*gh*, the navel. P. náf.
نال nál, horse shoe. A.
نام nám, name. P.
am-nám, namesake.
نانا náná, maternal grandfather. Si.
ناني náni, maternal grandmother. Si.
ناورش návarish, anything eaten as a relish with bread.
نبي nabí, prophet, A.
نپت napt, s. lightning. (Met.) a gun. (P. naft, naphtha.)
نپورغ nipúra*gh*, v., p.p. nipúra*th*a, to wring. Si. nipúṛanu.
نتهه nuth, s. face.
نخنبوخ na*kh*inbo*kh*, s. bedclothes; clothes given by a host to a guest.

نخيف na*kh*íf, slave.

نذخ na*dh*a*kh*, lemon-grass, (*Cymbopogon iwarancusa*).

نر nar, male. P.

نر nar, fife, pipe. Si. narí.

نرم narm, soft. P.

نروار nirwár, justice, decision of a disputed case. Si. nirwáru.

نريان naryán, a horse (m.).

نزکهنغ naz-khana*gh*, v. to close, bring together.

نزي nazí, } near. P. nazdík, nizd.
نزيخ nazí*kh*, }

نشار nishár, brother's wife; daughter-in-law. Skr. snushá. Pashto, nzhor.

نشان nishán, mark, standard. P.

نشتيجني nishtejaní, bedding.

نشتينغ nishtaina*gh*, to spread out. Causal of ninda*gh*.

نشک nashk, mark, sign, distinction. A. naqsha.

نغاه ni*gh*áh, sight, show. P. nigáh.

نغر nu*gh*ur. See no*gh*ar.

نغره nu*gh*ra, silver. P. nukra.

نغرئيفا nu*gh*raená, of silver.

نغن na*gh*an, bread. P. nán.

نغور ni*gh*or, side, direction.

نغوشغ ni*gh*osha*gh*. See nigosha*gh*.

نفا nafá, profit. A. nafa'.

نفسخ nafus*kh*, stepdaughter.

نکرا nukrá, white (of a horse). P.

نکرغ nikra*gh*, to separate, part (intr.).

نکل nakl, imitation, copying. A. naql.
nakl-khana*gh*, to imitate.

نکهه nakh, } old woman.
نکهو nakho, } ditto.

نگاه nigáh, care. P.

نگاه باني nigáhbání, carefulness.

نگوشغ nigosha*gh*, to listen, attend. Cf. Pashto, n*gh*watal.
p.p. nigoshtha.

نلي nalí, s. the forearm. Si. narí.
phá*dh*-nalí, the shin.

نلي nalí, s. the barrel of a gun. Si.

نماش namásh, prayers. P. namáz.

نمبو nambo, the búí plant, *Crotalaria burhia.*

نمبي nambí, s. fresh feeling in the air after rain.

نمک namak, in namak-harám, traitor. P.

نمونه namúna, pattern. P.

نگ nang, honor, dignity. P.

ننگار nangár, plough.
nangár baha*gh*, to plough.

ننڈغ ninda*gh*, v., p.p. nishtha, to sit, dwell, stay.
P. nishastan, nishín. Pashto, nástal.
er-ninda*gh*, to sit down.

نواسغ nawása*gh*, grandson, granddaughter. P. nawása.

نواشي nawáshí, to-morrow.
nawáshí-begá, to-morrow evening.

نوان nawá*n*, perhaps.

نوترين nautire*n*, a game resembling gobang, played on a board.

نوخ no*kh*, new. The new moon, the moon. P. nau.

نوخ nau*kh*, a bride. Pashto, náve.

نود nawad, felt. P. namda. Pahl. namad.

نوڈ no*dh*, rain clouds, rain.

نور nor, mungoose, ichneumon. S. noru.

نورا núrá, silver.

نوز navz, pulse. A. nafs.

نوزد núzd, } nineteen. P.
نوزده núzdah, }

نوغر no*gh*ar, or
نغر nu*gh*ur, } skirt of the hills.

نوک nok, beak of a bird. P.

نوکر naukar, servant. P.

نوکري naukarí, service. P.

نه nah, no, not. P.

نه nuh, nine. P.

نهر nahar, canal. A.

نهرم nuhram, ugly.

نهمت nahmat, intention. A.

نهمي nuhmí, ninth.

ني ní, } now. Pázand nu*n*. Pashto nan.
نين ní*n*, }

نياذغ nyá*dh*a*gh*, v., p.p. nyástha., to post, establish, appoint. P. nihádan.

نيام nyám, middle. P. miyán.
nyámá, in the middle.

نيامجي nyámjí, one who goes between, arbitrator.

نيامغ nyáma*gh*, middling, in the middle.

نيانوان nyá*n*wá*n*, in the middle, in (from nyámá).

نيت niyat, object, desire. A.

نيخ ne*kh*, good. P. nek.
ne*khen* du'á, prayer.

نيرموش nermosh, noon (for nem-rosh). P. nem-roz.

نيڑ níṛ, s. roast meat.

نيزغ neza*gh*, spear. P. neza.

نيستا nestá, } was not.
نيستث nesta*th*, }

نيستين neste*n*, is not.

نيستكار nestkár, poor, destitute. P.

نيش nesh, tooth. (Si. Pashto, neśh, tusk.)

نيغار ne*gh*ár, in the direction of. See nem*gha*.

نيكه nékah, marriage ceremony. A. nikáh.

نيلغ níla*gh*, blue.

نيم nem, half. P.

nem-ráh, halfway.

nem-shaf, midnight.

نیمغ nema*gh*, butter.

نیمغا nem*ghá*, in the direction of, towards.

نیمون nímon, lemon. A.

نین ne*n*, no, not.

نینه nína, modern, belonging to the present time.

nína-vakhat, now-a-days. See ní.

و W. V.

واجا wájá, } like, resembling.
واجهه wájh, }

وار wár. (In composition) eater. P. *kh*or.

mar-wár, man-eater.

shír-wár, suckling.

وارس wáris, heir. A. wári*th*.

واژا wázhá, lord, master, sir. P. *kh*waja.

di*gh*ár-wázhá, landlord.

lo*gh*-wázhá, goodman.

واگو vágú, a large lizard, alligator. (S. vághú, alligator.)

واگي vágí, that very one. S.

وام wám, debt.

وامدار wámdár, debtor.

وانج واپرا vánij-vápará, give and take, buying and selling (uncommon.) Si.

واندا wándá, leisure. Si. wándo.

وانغ wána*gh*, v., p.p. wántha, to read. P. *kh*wándan.

واهو wáhú, outcry, the alarm.

وباه wabáh, cholera. (Ar. wabá, pestilence.)

وپسغ wapsa*gh*, v., p.p. waptha., to sleep. P. *kh*uftan, *kh*usp.

وٹ waṭ, wick. Si. vaṭi.

وٹا waṭṭá, stone. Panj.

وتهي vitthí, space, interval. Si. vithí.

وث wa*th*, self, oneself. P. *kh*ud. Skr. swad-íya.

وثي wa*th*í, one's own, own.

وخت va*kh*t time. Ar. waqt.

وڈ waḍ, increase.

وڈاینغ vaḍáina*gh*, to increase. Panj. vaḍáwan.

وڈري vaḍrí, leather strap. Si. vaḍhí.

وڈري vaḍrí, bribery. Si. vaḍhí.

وذ wa*dh*. See وث wa*th*, self. P. *kh*ud.

وذي wa*dh*í, birth.

wa*dh*í khana*gh*, to foal.

وربريا warbaríyá, excellently, stoutly.

ورد ward, food.

ورغ wara*gh*, v., p.p. wártha, imp. bawar, to eat, drink. P. *kh*urdan. Skr. hvar.

ورنا warná, youth, young man. P. barná.

ورو warú, beam. Si. waro, rafter.

ورینغ waraina*gh*, causal of wara*gh*, to feed.

وس was, strength. Si. wasu.

be-was, helpless.

وسر wasar, wild onion. See whasar.

وستاد wastád, master of a subject, skilful. P. ustád.

وسرزاخت wasarzákht, brother-in-law. Cf. P. *kh*usar, záda.

وسرك wasarik, father-in-law. P. *kh*usar.

وسريا wasaríyá, in front, foremost.

وسم wasam, inhabited. Si. wasa*n*w.

وسي wasí, mother-in-law. P. khusú. Skr. çvaçrú.

وش wash, sweet, happy. P. *kh*ush. Skr. swádu.

وشكي washkí, male of any beast of chase.

وشي washí, sweetmeats.

وكيل vakíl, agent. A.

ول val,
ولان valán, creaper. Si. vali.

وني vanní, bride. Si.

وني vanní, name of a plant.
ونجغ vanija*gh*, v. to yield up.
ونيينغ vinyaina*gh*, v. to spoil. Si vinyáinu.
وهاذ whá*dh* or wahá*dh*, salt.
وهار whár, dirty, foul. P. *kh*or.
وهان whán, tray, dish. P. *kh*wan.
وهاو wháv, sleep. P. *kh*wáb. Z. qafna.
وهرد whard, food. P.
وهسر whasar, the wild onion, *Allium rubellium*. A.
ويس ves, clothing. Si. vesu.
ويلا velá, time. Si. velo.
ويهي vehí, street. Panj.

ه H.

هاجي hájí, pilgrim. A. حاجي.
هاخ há*kh*, earth, clay. P. *kh*ák.
هاذر há*dh*ir, heart. Ar. *kh*átir.
هارغ hára*gh*, dates. P. *kh*árik.
هازر házir, present, Ar. حاضر.
هاش hásh, double tooth. (Cf. Pashto *gh*áśh).
هاغا há*gh*á, awake.
هال hál, circumstances, new. A. حال.
hálá dai! give the news!
هالور hálwar, conversation.
هامغ háma*gh*, raw, unripe, uncooked. P. *kh*ám.
هان hán, khán, chief. P. *kh*án.
هباسي habásí, (عباي 'abbásí), an eight-anna piece.
هبر habar, discussion, conversation. P. *kh*abar.
هبكغ habka*gh*, v. to stutter. Si. habak.
هپت hapt, seven. P. haft.
هپتغ hapta*gh*, a week. P. haftá.

هپتمي haptumí, seventh. P.

هتر hatar, danger, apprehension. Ar. *kha*ṭar.

هٹ haṭ, shop. Si. haṭu.

هث ha*th*, the wild olive, *Olea cuspidata*. P. zaitún.

هچ huch, horse's hough. Si. khuch.

هچهو hachho, thus, so. P.

هچي hachí, any. Often contracted to 'chí. P. hech.

هديرغ hadíra*gh*, to chop up.

هڈ haḍ, bone. Si. haḍu. Pashto, haḍ.

هڈكي hiḍkí, hiccough. Si. hiḍikí. Pashto haṭkaí.

هذا hu*dh*á, } God. P. *kh*udá.
هذاي hu*dh*ái, }

هذين ha*dh*en, then.

هر hir, a young male camel up to six months.

هر har, every, each. P.

har-do, both.

har-rangá, of every kind.

har-ro, daily, always.

har-sál, every year.

har-kas, every one.

har-ki, every thing that—, each.

har-va*kh*tá, } always.
har-velá, }

har-handá, everywhere.

هر hur, adv. apart.

hur-jana*gh*, to drag apart.

هرب harb, jawbone.

هرتال hartál, arsenic. (Si. hartálu, yellow orpiment.)

هرتيل hartel, large saddle bags.

هرجين hurjín, saddle bags. P. *kh*urjí.

هردك hirdik, squirrel.

هردهات hardhát, metal. Skr. dhátu.

هرس hirs, avarice. A.

هرش harsh,
هرشه harsha, } a cubit.

هرغ harra*gh*, s. an infirm person.

هرغ harra*gh*, s. a saw.

هرف harf, letter. Ar.

هرمزاده harmzáda, bastard, scoundrel. A. P.

هرنولي harnolí, dhatura.

هروار harwár, a measure of corn containing nearly 10 maunds Indian weight. P. *kh*arwár.

هري harrí,
هريا harriyá, } mad (of dogs).

هژده hazhdah, eighteen. P.

هژگر hizhgar, anywhere.

هس has, an ornament, a "hassí" or silver necklace. Si. hasu.

هستل hastal, mule.

هشت hasht, eight. P.

هشتر hushtur, camel, (the generic term). P. shutur.
Skr. ushṭra. Brahui huch. Zend. ustra. Pashto ú*sh*.

هشتمي hashtumí, eighth.

هشغ husha*gh*, p.p. hushtha, to dry (intr.).

هشک hushk, dry. P. *kh*ushk. Skr. çushká. Z. huska.
hushke*n* ḍoḍ, skeleton.

هشکي hishkí, scarlet.

هک hak, rights.

هکل hakal, drawing.

هکلغ hakala*gh*, v., p.p. hakala*th*a, to drive, to urge on.

هکم hukm, (A. ḥukm), order.

هل hal, melting; hal bía*gh*, to melt, thaw.

هل hil, a kite. Si.

هلاس hulás, free. P. *kh*ulás.

هلك halk, village, collection of huts. (Cf. Ar. *kh*alk, *kh*alkat.)

هليذ hale*dh*, spices.

هليذي halení, adv. undoubtedly.

همباچه hambácha, ammunition pouch. Si. hambácho.

همبار hambár, a collection of corn, and enclosure round it. P. ambár.

هموذا hamo*dh*á, there, in that very place.

هميذا hame*dh*á, here, in this very place.

هميش hamesh, this very one.

hameshiya phar, on this account.

هن han, neighing, whinnying.

han-khana*gh*, to neigh, whinny.

هنجري hinjrí, the shoulder-blade. See bardast. Si. hanjhí.

هنجير hinjír, fig. (P. anjír.)

هنچهو hanchho, thus, so. P.

هند hand, s. place, dwelling. (P. *kh*ána.) (Si. handhu.)

handá, in place, instead.

thí-handá, elsewhere.

har-handá, everywhere.

hech-handá, anywhere.

hech-handá ne*n*, nowhere.

handiyá, somewhere.

ya-handá, in one place, together.

ás-hand, fire-place.

zahm-hand, scar of a sword-wound.

هند hind, bitch.

هندي hindí, weapon.

هندينغ handaina*gh*, to be useful.

هنر hunar, skill.

هنكغ hinka*gh*, to neigh.

هنگر hangar, charcoal. (Cf. Sindhi a*ng*aru.)

هنگلو hingalo, variegated. (Si. hingulú vermilion.)

هو hau, yes.

هوان hawán, that. (P. ham-án.)

هوانكر hawánkar, as much as that.

هوانگو hawángo, thither.

هوت hot, hero, warrior.

هود haud, tank. Ar.

هوده havdah, seventeen. P.

هوده دار hodadár, official (for P. uhdadár).

هوڈ hoḍ, hole, cave, den.

هور haur, rain. Si. horu.

هور hor,
هورگ horg, } empty.
هورگین horgín,

هورجین horjín. See hurjín. Saddle bags.

هوش hosh, sense. P.

هوشغ hosha*gh*, s. an ear of corn. (P. *kh*osha.)

هوشیار hoshyár, skilful. P.

هوف hauf, leprosy; a severe illness, violent fever.

هول hol,
هول پوش hol-posh, } armour, accoutrements. Si.

هوم hom, the air-plant.

هون hon, blood. P. *kh*un.

هویش hawesh, this, this one.

هوین hawe*n*, adj. this.

هي ḥí. See hí*dh*ishk.

هي hai, or.

hai hai, either, or. (P. *kh*wáh, *kh*wáh.)

هیا hayá, shame. A.

be-hayá, shameless.

هیت hait, camel's pack-saddle.

هیث hí*th*, green corn, khasíl. P. *kh*awíd.

هیچ hech, any. P.

هیچي hechí, anything.

hechí na,
'chí na, } nothing, none, not at all.

هیخ hí*kh*, swine. P. *kh*úk.

هیذ he*dh*, sweat. (Skr. svid. P. pa-sína.)

هیذ شک hí*dh*ishk, the khip bush, *Orthanthera viminea.*

هیر hír, a houri. (Ar. ḥúr.)

هیر hair, welfare, (Ar. *kh*air.)

hair khana*gh*, to salute.

ma-hairá, all's well.

هیران hírán, dish, plate.

هیرتهه hírth, fine, thin.

هیزه haiza, cholera.

هیژوخ hízho*kh*, a waterfall.

هیس hes, rust, dirt.

هیل híl, hope.

هیلاك helák, tame, subdued, accustomed. Si. heráku.

هیلوند hílwand, hopeful.

هینز hí*n*z, a leather churn.

hí*n*zár matha*gh*, to churn.

هینه hína, weak. Si. hiṇo.

ي Y.

یاژده yázhdah, eleven. P.

یاژدمي yázhdumí, eleventh. P.

یتیم yatím, orphan. A.

یکین yakín, certain. A.

یک yak, one. P.

yak-áptiyá, one another.

yake, only one.

yake-chyár, fourfold, } &c.
yake-sai, threefold, }

یله دیغ yala dea*gh*, to let loose. See الغ دیغ ila*gh* dea*gh*.
Pashto, yalah.

یمارا yamárá, for ever. See jamárá.

یه ya, one. Cf. Pashto yau, yavah.

ya-bará, at once.

ya-bare, once.

ya-rangá, of one sort.

ya-handá, in one place, together.

SPECIMENS

OF

THE BALOCHI LANGUAGE.

I.

The Wanderings of the Rind Balochís.

[This poem is very widely spread, and I have met with it in almost every Baloch tribe. The versions differ very slightly. The present one, as the dedication in the last two lines shows, was recited to Jalál *Kh*án a former Chief of the Le*gh*árís. Another version, from a Gurchání Ḍom, similarly brings in the name Nihál *Kh*án. The poem is probably of considerable age; it is very elliptical in expression, many of the grammatical forms are antiquated, and the versification is loose and formless. It gives the legendary account of the Wanderings of the Baloches before they settled in the countries they now inhabit, distinguishes the tribes entitled to rank as Rinds from those not so entitled, and concludes with a catalogue of their leaders.]

Shukr Alláh hamdá guzárá
    badsháh mulka wa*th*e*n*
Thí jihán *kh*ák o gilo bí
    Heku nindo wash-dilá.
Má auládí Mír Hamzái*gh*-ú*n*
    Sob dargáhá gur e*n*
Azh Halabá phá*dh* kháyá*n*
    go jazízá*n* jheroe*n*
Masará Míre*n* Jalál Há*n*
    chhil-o-chyár bolak e*n*
Kalabalá Bompúr ma-nyá*n*wá*n*
    shahr Shistán mizile
Khá*kh*tú*n* Hárína bandá
    Kech ráste*n* phalawá

Makuráná Hot nindí
    Khosa*gh* ma*n* Kech-dehá
Azh Halabá Chánḍiye*gh*á
    Kalamthí e lo*gh* pha-gure*n*
Jo mítáf bahr-khanána
    Kul sardár Shaihak e*n*
Ma*n* Nalíyá Noh nindí
    Jistkání pha-gure*n*
Phuzh, Mírali, Jatoí
    Drust ma*n* Seví Ḍháḍará
Dríshak *Khán*, Mazárí
    E go Rindá yagsar e*n*
Azh bunyádá Phuzh Rinde
    Sar go Mír e*n* Chákur e*n*
Golo, Gopáng, Dashti
    Rind thalíyá dar-ant
Thí Baloch báz bisháre*n*
    Drust ma*n* Rindá manahá
Nashk-daur pha Gorgezá*n*
    E ma*n* Thalíyá dehá
Noh korái áwáre*n*
    E go Rindá yagsare*n*
Rindá*n* ma*n* Shorán nindí
    Láshar ma*n* Gandáva*gh* e*n*
E maní perá o rand e*n*
    E Balocha daptar e*n*
Má deú*n* sí sál jangá
    E Balocha shiddat e*n*
Shaihak o Sháhdád dání
    Las sardár Chákar e*n*
Chhil hazár khái Mír gwá*n*khá
    Thewa*gh*á*n* ḍáḍe-potar e*n*
Hol-posh dast-kaláyá
    Druh khawán o jábah e*n*
Paṭh pechá go khawá
    Phá*dh* lále*n* mozha*gh* e*n*
Kárch kátar nu*gh*raená
    Dast mundrí thangave*n*
Bakar o Gwaharám Rámena
    Zar-zuwál No*dh* banda*gh* e*n*
Phuzhá*n* Járo jaur-jawáv e*n*
    Hadde*n* Díne brá*dh*ar e*n*

Pheroz o Bijar Rehán
    Mírán Rindá*n* zahm-jan e*n*
Sohbá, Míhán, Alí,
    Jám, Sahák o Alan e*n*
Haivtá*n* Bívara*gh* ma*n* Rindá*n*
    Mír Hassan go Brahim e*n*
Sháir ki sherá*n* jorí
    Mír Jalál Há*n* surpha*dh* e*n*.

Translation.

Thanks and praise to God; himself he is Lord of the land. When the rest of the word becomes dust and clay, alone He remains with serene heart.

We are the offspring of Mír Hamza; victory is in the worship of God. From Halab do we arise, there are fights with the unbelievers. Foremost is Mír Jalál *Kh*án, there are four and forty tribes. By stages (we march) from Kalabalá (Karbalá?) to Bompúr and the cities of Sístán. We came to Hárún's band, on the right side of Kech. The Hots settle in Makrán, the Khosas in the land of Kech. From Halab come the Chánḍyas, near the home of the Kalamthís. Dividing out running water and dry land, the chief of all is Shaihak.

In Nalí the Nohs settle, close to the Jistkánís. The Phuzhes, Míralís and Jatoís, all in Seví and Ḍháḍar. The Drishaks, Kháns and Mazárís are one with the Rinds. In origin the Phuzhes are Rinds, they were with Mír Chákar. The Golos, Gopángs and Dashtís are outside the Rind circle (dish). The other very numerous Baloches are all included in the Rinds. Distinguished for wealth among the Gorgezes are those in the country of Thalí. The Nohs and Korais are mixed together, they are one with the Rinds. The Rinds settle in Shorán, the Lashárís in Gandává. This is our foot-print and track, this is the Baloch record. For thirty years we are engaged in battle, this is the Baloch struggle.

In the time of Shaihak and Sháhdád, Chákar was chief of the whole. Forty thousand come at the Mir's call, all descendants of one ancestor. All with armour upon their forearms, all with bows and quivers; with silk scarves and overcoats, and red boots on their feet; with silver knives and daggers, and golden rings on their hands. There were Bakr and Gwaharám and Rámen, and the gold-scattering No*dh*banda*gh*. Of the Phuzhes was Járo, venemous in reply, and Hadde his brother by religion. There were Pheroz, Bijar, Rehán, and Míran, the swordsman of the Rinds. There were Sohbá, Míhá*n*, Ali, Jám, Ishák and Alan; Haibat Hán and Bívara*gh* of the Rinds, and Mír Hassan with Bráhim.

It is the poet that composes the songs, and Mír Jalál *Kh*án comprehends them.

II.

Poems relating to Mír Chákar.

Mír Chákar is the great legendary hero of the Rind Baloches. He is represented as having led them into the countries they now occupy from Makrán, and as having founded a kingdom with its capital Sevi (Síbí). He waged war with the Turks under Humáú Chu*gh*attá. On the civil war between the Rinds and Lasháris breaking out, the Turks under their leader Zunú joined the Rinds, and the Lasháris were defeated. The Turks seized the Lashári women, but released them on the expostulation of Chákar, who said that Baloches would be disgraced by being accomplices in such a deed. At one time Chákar was a prisoner to Humáú, who called him up and asked him "What is the best of all weapons?" Chákar replied, "Anything that a man can lay hold of in a fight." The king then had Chákar brought unarmed into a narrow street, and a savage elephant turned loose at the other end. As it rushed upon Chákar, he caught up a dog that was lying in the road, and threw it in the elephant's face with such violence that it turned and fled. Chákar is said to have founded the old fort at Síbí, which he ultimately abandoned at the end of the civil war on his way to the Panjáb. His name has been given to several places in Balochistán, among them Chákar-márí 'Chákar's upper storey,' a hill near Sangsíla in the Bugtí country, from which he is said to have taken his last look back at Síbí. This is a physical impossibility, but Chákar was a 'godlike man' (Hu*dh*ái mard), and could do things which the present generation is not capable of. Another place, named after him, is Chákar Tankh 'Chákar's defile' in the Marrí country.

It is difficult to say how far any part of Chákar's adventures are historical. Baloches began to arrive at Multán and the neighbourhood from Makrán in the time of Hussain Langá, towards the end of the 15th century. (Briggs' Ferishta, Vol. IV, p. 388.) Soon afterwards came one whose name is transliterated by Briggs Meer Jakur Zund, which should probably be Mír Chákar Rind. He obtained a jágír in Uchh from Jám Báyazíd (Ib. p. 396).

This Mír Chákar is said to have come from Solypur, but I have not been able to discover this place. This was about 1520 A. D. About the same time we find Baloches in the Panjáb as far north as Babrah and Khusháb on the Jehlam. (Erskine's Baber, p. 256.)

This irruption of Baloches into the Panjáb was probably caused by the pressure on them of the Turks or Mu*gh*als who were then under the *Argh*úns invading Kachhí and Sindh. Sháh Beg, son of Zúlmún Beg *Argh*ún, took Síbí first in A. D. 1479 and a second time about A. D. 1511. This occupation may have been the cause of Chákar's emigration. Sháh

Beg made Síbí his capital for some time, and it is probable that he and not Chákar really built the old fort there (Erskine's Baber and Humáyún. Ed. 1854, Vol. I, pp. 342, 347, 348.) There is no record of any collision between Humáyún and the Baloches except during his flight in A. D. 1543, when he seems to have been plundered by them in the Bolán Pass. (Baber and Humáyún, Vol. II. p. 266) and again fell in with them between Kandahár and Sístán (p. 271). This is perhaps sufficient for the introduction of his name into the legends. Zunú, the Turk leader, perhaps stands for Zúlnún Beg in whose name Sháh Beg fought.

The Quarrel of Mír Chákar and Gwaharám.

[This poem also seems from its language to be an old one. It describes the causes of the division between the Rinds and Lasháris, the two sections into one of which all true Baloches fall. The Rinds were under Chákar, the Lasháris under Gwaharám. Finally Chákar in disgust emigrated to the Panjáb, and settled at Satghar in the Lahore District, where he died and is said to be buried.]

Kilátí Havív gushí: Sarí Rind *Gh*ulám Bolak gushí: Chákar Gwaharám Karákuṭán gushí: Gohar báutíyá kharde gál gushí: philave*n* sí-sál-jang gushí.

Yád khanán náme Iláhí
man awwal sar-náva*gh*á*n*
Haidar o phusht o phanáh
sar hazrate á*kh*ir-zamá*n*
Biyá lorí go sawáhá
zír maní guftára*gh*á*n*
Bar gwara belá*n* dile*gh*á
no salátí brá*dh*ará*n*.
Mangehá Rinda pha Bompur
Kech bá*gh*e Makurá*n*
Mastare*n* lo*gh* Domkí e*n*
ma*n* Balochi meravá*n*
Rind Láshárí áwárá
trán bastha pha-wa*th*á*n*
'Biyáe*th*, she*dh*á bilaḍú*n*
bilú*n* giyáfe*n* ulkahá*n*
Jo mítáfá bi-kaṭú*n*
bahr-khanú*n* bi pha wa*th*á*n*.

Rájí ráná ka*dh* ma lekú*n* '
biyá*kh*thá*n* da*n* lo*gh* gi*th*á*n*
Hukmí ṭonḍe na*kh*ífá*n*
no*kh* khu*th*antesh ádimá*n*
Bozh borá*n* báṛa*gh*ená
kotwání andará
Saj khane báze*n* bihána
nuh-hazárí markhavá*n*
Biyárú*n* bagá*n* girda*gh*ená
azh Naliya khaur dafá
Gwánkh-ja*th*a jo*dh*á*n* bi káḍá*n*
'er-khafe azh Chajuá
Khash gálí o palangá
jhul suhre*n* kamalá*n*
Bauf morbande*n* lihefá*n*
hingaloe*n* manjavá*n*
Sikh o tásá*n* bijore*n*
Makuráni kadahá*n*
Chakurí deh na nindí.
ro wa*th*í díre*n* ámilá*n*.'
Phoshi*th*a Rindá*n* wa*th*í díṛ
pha khawáh o shaddavá*n*
Phá*dh* lále*n* mozha*gh*á*n*
Rind kása*th*ant pha Deravá*n*
Ḍháḍar o Seví gwáftha
Da*n* Jhal o Nílahá dafá,
Hab, Phab, Moh, Malí
da*n* Nalí khaur dafá
Gáj shahra bastha*gh*ená
Da*n* Marágaho dehá
Sangar o khoh Sulemá
Gwáftha*gh*en sher-nará*n*
Sáng Mundáhí dhaníyá
Ḍan pá bi Me*th*irá
Bá*gh*chae*n* Kácho Símá
Da*n* Dharí o Bhanará
Nangare Bijár the*gh*á
Jám Sulemána lurá.
Gohar báutí ki á*kh*tha
gwar Nawáve Chákurá
'Mál maní othíya bag e*n*
hande phe-dáre maná*n*'

Chákurá dír-zána*gh*ená
    gwash bi durre*n* Gohará
'Barav o Során joá
    Kachrákí phalavá,
He-miuná bagá bichárе*n*,
    nind be-ande*n* shafá.'
Rosh azh Gwaharám shahrá
    rafttha*gh*ant kharde chariá*n*
Bára*gh*e*n* borá*n* zawárant
    pha shikár o sailahán.
Hir khushthant jufta*gh*íyá
    phar wa*th*í láf-serihá*n*
Ráj bundá*th*ant hazárí
    azh du-demí ziánehá
Kahravá theká*n* khawáthant
    pha ba*dh*e*n* kirdára*gh*á*n*
'Shin-gurá Gwaharám the*gh*á
    'shán-gurá Mír Chákurá
Phílave*n* sí sál jang a*th*
    Gohara hir pha*dh*á
Sar galoí bái*th*a*gh*antí
    nesh ri*kh*thant azh dafá
Márá dí ekhawá dí ishtha
    pha Hu*dh*ái ásurá
Guḍá Sultáne Balochá
    sahl khu*th*a bi pha wa*th*á*n*
Chákur azh brá*th*í gasúrá.
    Gwastha Satte*n* Ghará*n*.

Translation.

Kiláti son of Habíb says: to the lofty Ghulám Bolak Rinds he says; about the quarrel between Chákar and Gwaharám he says: of the refuge-taking of Gohar in few words he says: of full thirty years war he says, as follows:

First I remember the name of God, my morning-star of old; lord, and support and protector to the most illustrious prophet.

Come minstrel at early morn, learn my sayings and carry them to the friends of my heart, and the assembly of my brethren.

The bold Rinds came to Bompúr, to Kech and fertile Makrán, the greatest family was the Domkí in the Baloch assemblies.

The Rinds and Lasháris met together, they took counsel among themselves. "Come, let us march hence, let us leave these widespread lands. Let us conquer streams and dry lands, and deal them out among ourselves. Let us take no count of rule or ruler."

They came to their own homes. The chiefs (turban-wearers) ordered their slaves to saddle their young mares. "Loose the slender chestnut (mares) from their stalls, saddle the numerous fillies, steeds worth nine-thousand each. Let us bring in herds of camels from round about, from the mouth of the torrent of Nalí." The men called to the women "Come down from Chajú, take out your wrappings and beds, carpets and red blankets, pillows, and spotted rugs, and many-coloured bedsteads, moulded cups in abundance, and Makrání drinking vessels. Chákar will not stay in this country, he will go to his own far land."

The Rinds clothed their bodies in overcoats and turbans, with red boots on their feet. The Rinds were distinguished for hospitality.

They called together Ḍháḍar and Seví, in Jhal and the mouth of the Nílah; Hab, Phab, Moh and Malí in the mouth of the Nalí torrent. They stayed at the city of Gáj in the land of Marágah. The tigers of men assembled Sangar and the Sulaiman mountains, the rulers of Sáng and Mundáhí became payers of tribute to our chief.

In the boundaries of fertile Kachhí, in Dharí and Bhanar. There was generous Bíjar with his scimitar, and the leader Sulaimán with his sword.

Gohar came for refuge with the Nawáb Chákar, saying "Show me a place for my cattle, and herds of camels." The far-seeing Chákar said to the fair Gohar "Go to the streams of Shorau in the direction of Kachrak. There stay at ease with your herds of camels, and have no anxiety by night."

One day some madmen went forth from Gwaharám's city, they were mounted on fine chestnut (mares), for the sake of hunting and exercise.

They killed a pair of young camels (of Gohar's), to fill their bellies withal.

The chief fell into a great rage (lit. rage of a thousand), on both sides damage was done. A curse falls upon the wicked, upon the doers of evil. On this side was Gwaharám with his sword, on that side Mír Chákar. For full thirty years war continued about these young camels of Gohar's. All the excellent youths have been slain, the teeth have dropped from their mouths, and God's mercy has spared us only. Then the Baloch rulers made peace among themselves, and Chákar on account of this feud among brethren passed away to Satghar.

Chákar's denunciation of his foes on leaving Síbí.

Chákar Shaihak gushí: sarí Rind Bádsháh gushí: *á*n rosh ki Seví khilí kharde gál gushí: Gwaharámár phasave dá*th* gushí.

Bilá*n* mar-lawáshe*n* Seví
Gaure*n* sa*dh*aní margáví
Jáme Nindavá bhaṭṭiyá
Sai-roshá*n* Baharám ne*gh*á
Sí-sál uvt o uzhmárá
Ján-jebhavá*n* jangiyá
The*gh* azh balgavá honená
Chotá*n* cho kamándí bo*gh*á*n*
. Ju*kh*tán na nashant lárená
Warnáyá*n* du-manḍílená.
Laḍ ma ḍeravá*n* na rusthaut
Misk ma barútá*n* na mushthant
Whard dumbag*h*á*n* mesháni
Karwálí sharáb sharr joshant
Shábán pha nishán yakhe nest
Drustá*n* wártha*gh*á*n* hindíyá*n*
Shartá*n* dá*th*a*gh*á*n* shímená*n*
Bachaki lawar bá*n*zíyá
Gwaharám muzhe*n* Gandáva*gh*
Singhe ma zirih phirentha
Máchíya lawáshtha lanjaíth
Alí o Walí druh-dárá*n*
Yákí kiláta berone*n*
Há*gh* kávalí Turkáná*n*
Rind bára*gh*e*n* borá*n*á*n*
Gwaharám azh dude hande bí
Ne Gor bí ne Gandáva*gh*.

Translation.

Chákar son of Shaihak says: the exalted Ruler of the Rinds says: on the day he leaves Síbí these few words he says: in reply to Gwaharám he says (as follows):

I will leave man-devouring Seví, curses on my infidel foes! For three days shall the Jám Nindo from his oven (distribute bread) in honour of Bahrám (slain). For thirty years, for ever shall there be war with these gigantic men, nor shall my sword be clean from stains of blood. I will bend it like jointed sugarcane, so that through crookedness it will not go into the sheath.

The distinguished (lit. two-turbaned) youths do not rise up to sport among the houses, they rub no scent on their moustaches, but they eat fat-tailed sheep and boil strong liquor in their stills. There is not one of them with signs of a ruler about him. They have eaten all their weapons, they have gambled away their heads, they have children's sticks in their hands. Let Gwaharám stay in dusty Gandáva, a stone thrown into a well. Máchí has drunk blood; Alí and Walí are traitors. The rebels' fort has been surrounded, and reduced to earth by the tyrannous Turks and the Rinds on highbred mares (chestnuts). Gwaharám (will be expelled) from both places, (and possess) neither a grave nor Gandáva.

III.

Dosten and Shíren.

The legend on which the following poem is based is as follows:

During the war between Mír Chákar the Rind leader and Humáú Chu*gh*attá king of the Turks (*i. e.* the Bádsháh Humáyún), Chákar was forced to consent to give up some Rind maidens to Humáú, but actually sent instead young men in disguise. On this being discovered, they were ordered to be kept in perpetual imprisonment in the fort of Harrand. Among these prisoners was Dosten. He had been engaged to marry his cousin Shíren, who remained faithful to him during his many years' imprisonment. At last her parents said that she must no longer remain unmarried, no hope being left of Dosten's return; so they found for her another husband, also named Dosten. (This is alluded to in line 98, where she says 'Not this Dosten, but the old one.') Him she long refused to marry, but at last yielded to the pressure put on her, and arrangements were made for the ceremony. Meanwhile Dosten in prison at Harrand had succeeded in gaining the favour of the Mu*gh*al or Turk Governor of the fort, and some liberty was allowed him. His mare had died, but had first borne a fine colt which had grown up, and which Dosten was allowed to keep. One day games and races were going on, and Dosten asked and obtained leave to join in the race. Mounting his horse, he said good-bye to the Governor, turned its head towards the Cháchar Pass and went off at full speed. Several pursuers followed him, but no horse had the endurance of his chestnut. At intervals along the rocky pass they stumbled and fell, and these spots bear the horses' names to the present day. At last he was left alone, having wearied out all his pursuers, and travelled homewards. On nearing his tribe, he overtook a minstrel (Ḍom or lorí). He asked him the news, and where he was going. The minstrel told him of the impending marriage of Shíren, and said that he was on his way to sing at the wedding. Dosten then told his story and prevailed on the minstrel to change clothes with him. Thus disguised, he made his way into the assembly with the other minstrels, and sang the poem which follows, bringing in the substance of a message he had received in captivity from Shíren. He was immediately recognized by Shíren, who declared that she would marry him and no other, and they were happily married then and there.

In the poem Dosten first begins by saying how his mare could not live in the heat of the plains, and then passes on to say how a *Kh*orásán merchant brought him down Shíren's message, which constitutes the remainder of the poem. It begins with an animated description of a Nomadic Baloch tribe in the hills moving to fresh pastures after rain, and then turns to Shíren weeping in her little hut for her lost lover. Her companions try to console her, but she will not be consoled, since he is in captivity. She then describes how when she wanders over the hills with the other Baloch women, according to their custom, she always picks a flower for her lover's sake, and ends with a prayer for his safe return home again.

Lines 40-44 seem to be an interpolation. They have no connexion with the subject matter of the poem.

Zangí maní badero
Gwaharám maní jám o bel
Whántkár Shíhane Sháhiye
Sau*gh*an pha thaí risháná
No*khí*-*ákh*tha*ghen* masáná
Sí*ghen* gor-khushe*n* syábhárá
*Á*fa na wárth Báh ne*ghá*
Kikh o Karjalá*n* Sinde*ghán*
Loṭí báhirá*n* Dashte*ghán*
Loṭí wa*dh*-maháre*n* jí*dhán*
Phito*kh* dafá má*dh*-gorá*n*
Ḍorí phur kumáre*n* áfá
Sutí phurí khaiává*n*
Whává kálrá nelá*n*
Máṛwáṛí jawá*n* zivirená*n*
Marde azh Hurásán *ákh*tha
Le*gh*ár chádar o humboe*n*
Bár ro*dh*kanání gona*th*
Hurjín mai*dhen* bhangání
Sarbár Kandahárí miskant
Phai*gh*ám gon-a*thí* Rindání

Tahkíke*n* shalám Shírene.
No*dh*á*n* shanz-ja*th*a Konárá
Dasht-o-dámana Mungáchar
Sanniya nu*gh*or humboe*n*
Ḍor phurant-í amrezá*n*
Larzant cho gwanání thá*kh*á*n*
Chotant cho kawándí bo*gh*á*n*.
Laḍí mánchá*th*a máldárá*n*
Meshí buzí whántkárá*n*
Mezhdár Sahák Yárá*n*
Bumbár bastha*gh*an bánukhá*n*
Sarbár láṛi*th*an gwánechá*n*
Bháwanar khanda*gh* o Nágáhú
Khondá*n* phrushtha*gh*an zardoá*n*
Loká*n* phashaví katárá*n*
Káḍá*n* go himáre*n* phá*dh*á*n*
Shírená ja*th*a srá*dh*e*n* kul
Ma Narmukh geáve*n* rejá.
Mesh azh draniná ser kha*n*
Buz azh gwári*gh*á lál phulá
Rind azh mai*dh*e*n* gandímá
Pah*n*wál azh phanír ponchá
Lahri azh gwan phothá*kh*á
Gwán' janth dilsare*n* dáiyá
Zirí kadahe meṭeí
Ro da shakhale*n* no*kh*áfá
Malgor shustha*gh*e*n* mahlíjá
Randí*th* mushi malgorá*n*
Khaithí da wa*th*í chyár-kulá
Kullá darríya bandí
Shiskant tha*gh*ard nishthent-í
Jhul phalavá leṭení
Dast janth avr barziyá
Khashí nu*gh*rae*n* ádená
Era Kamálú sar záná
Gindí droshamá heriyá
Gre*gh* khant humáre*n* chhamá
Anzí ríshant pha dramá
Jí*gh* sar katiká mená
Much ban janá*n* jedí gohár
Sharre*n* somare*n* chhil-o-chyár
Biáyant o gwara er-nindant
Shár phalavá leṭená

Phursant-í dila o hálá.
'Pharche khunalat khordema
Suhre*n* ma*n* ma*kh* o níláná
Brí*kh* thaí bambave*n* da*n*zená'
Gre*gh* bí*th*, janá*n* telánk dá*th*
'Dír bí*th*, o janá*n*, jawán e ná
Dir bí*th*, o janán, dír ninde
Bilá*n* khunal o khor-demá
Suhrá*n* ma*n* ma*kh* o nílá bant
Brí*kh* o bambave*n* da*n*ze*n* bant
Dost shume phakár ne*n*
*Kn*mar ki jána dozwáhá
Suhrá reá darkárá
Dí*th*a harra*gh*e*n* bad-duáyá*n*
Turká*n* azh hareb gwázentha
Ma zar-joshe*n* Arandá shahrá
Sunje*n* isp-tah'ale*n* láfá.'
Dúng bant janikh Rindá*n*í
Maláni pha*dh*á shef ban.
Kháyant khargazí krámáná
Ne*kh*e*n*-niyate*n* gwandáná.
Maurá*n* azh kurmá*n* sindáná
Phaṭá*n* gwára*gh*í lálphulá*n*
Nem jamaven jí*gh*a jant
Nem khunal o sar-hoshá*n*
Nem pha sammáe*n* khauliyá
Yakhe pha maní níyatá
Chi*th*o ma wa*th*í musht khan'
Ba phusht azh ba*dh*á*n* jaurená
'Shí*th* daz-gohár jeḍiyá
Dastá*n* pha Hu*dh*á burzáre
'Alláh ki biyár Malik Dostená
Saute*n* sammáe*n* khauliyá
Eshiyá ná, hawá*n* oliyá
Bor pha lamma*gh*á*n* sheriyá*n*
Baro mizilá*n* dírená
Biyár wázhá amírená
Nind-o-nyá*dh* phi*th*-o-má*th*ání
Dímá shakhale*n* brá*th*ání
Rozí bá Malik Dostená
Dídár khasha rozí bá.

Translation.

Zangí is my chief, Gwabarám my leader and friend, the owner of excellent mares. I swear by your beard, by the new grown hair of your face. My mare, hunter of wild asses, is sad, she will not drink water by the Indus, nor eat the reeds and karjal grass of Sind. She longs for the herds of wild asses of the Dasht, she longs for her own pleasant pastures, for the female wild asses of the Phito*kh* Pass, and the pools full of fresh water; the sandflies and musquitos irritate her, the vermin will not let her sleep, the Máṛwáṛí barley is coarse to her.

A man came from *Kh*orásán, his clothes and face dirty; he brought with him loads of madder, saddle-bags of fine bhang, and bales of Kandahár musk.

He had with him a message from the Rinds, a true greeting from Shíren.

The clouds have rained on Konár, on the plain and hill-skirts of Mungáchar, on the pleasant slopes of Sanní.

The pools are filled to over-flowing, (the water) trembles like the leaves of the gwan-tree (*Pistacia khinjuk*), and bends like joints of sugar-cane. The graziers have given the word to march, the owners of the sheep and goats, Mezhdár, Sahák and Yár Khán; the housewives have tied up their bundles, the camel-drivers have loaded their bales. On the hill-passes of Bháwnar and Nágáhú, the yellow camels bend their knees, the male camels in long strings, the women with tender feet. Shíren has pitched her fair tent on the wide spreading land of Narmukh.

Feed the sheep on dranin-grass, the goats on red-flowered gwári*gh*, the Rinds on wheaten flour, the shepherds on curds, and the Lahrís on gwan-berries.

She calls her beloved nurse and takes up an earthen cup, she goes to the sweet, fresh water, and her handmaiden washes her hair. She combs and smooths her hair and comes to her four-sided hut. She closes the door of the hut. They plait and spread the matting, and she reclines on the carpet.

She puts her hand into her bag and takes out a silver mirror, rests it on her shapely thigh and looks at her houri-like countenance. She weeps with her tender eyes, tears drop upon her cheeks and on her variegated breast-garment. Her companions and sisters assemble, fair comrades forty and four; they come and sit down by her, they recline upon blankets, they ask after her heart and condition.

They say, "Why are your face and earrings uncleaned, your red and blue clothes unwashed, your locks unkempt and dusty?" Weeping, she pushes the women away and says, "Away from here, women, you are not good. Away! sit far off! Let my face and earrings be uncleaned, my red and blue clothes unwashed, my locks tangled and dusty; I do not want you for friends. He who was the friend of my heart, for whose sake I should adorn myself, I saw carried off from his native land by evil cursed Turks, shut up in the wealthy city of Harraud, within an empty stable.

The daughters of the Rinds form a band, (and wander) following in the track of the showers. The vultures come croaking, invoking good fortune. Breaking the Maur-flowers from their stems, and plucking the red gwáragh flowers, some place them in their boddices and breasts, some in their earrings, lower and upper, and some (keep them) for their true love's sake. Pluck one for my good luck, and keep it in your closed hand; and, secretly from my bitter foes, my own sister and love says, with hands raised up to God. "May God bring back Malik Dosten, according to his true promise, not this one, but the old one. Swiftly, tiger-like chestnut mare, bear him southwards, come by long stages, bring home my noble lord to dwell with his father and mother and the assembly of his beloved brethren. May Malik Dosten appear, may he appear to my sight.

NOTES ON THE TEXT.

The text of this poem is taken from two versions, one recited by a Shambání, the other by a Marrí. There are some variations which are noted below, the Shambání version being marked (*a*), the Marrí version (*b*). The Shambání version is the base of the text. A fragment marked (*c*) from a Gurchání Dom supplies a line or two.

Lines 10 and 15 are supplied from (*c*).

Line 11 is only found in (*b*) and (*c*).

Line 18. For ro*dh*ananí (*b*) reads mehlaváni 'spices.'

Line 27. Larzant is from (*b*). (*a*) reads drafshant.

Line 32. For bánukhá*n* (*b*) reads godiyá*n*, with the same meaning.

Lines 40—44 appear to be interpolated. They only occur in (*a*), which contains several passages not in the other version.

Lines 46—48 are from (*b*). The whole passage from line 45 to line 57 is almost identical with one in the poem of Lailí and Majnún. Lines 56 and 57 are from (*b*).

(*a*) reads: 'Phulle*n* zán sará er-khant
Gindí azh wa*th* o gonáfá

Line 62 is from (*b*). (*a*) reads 'Hírth jedirí chhil o chyár'

Line 68. For da*n*zená (*b*) reads be-zau*n*k-an, 'unornamented.'

Line 69. For gre*gh* bí*th* 'weeps' (*b*) reads zahr gírth 'is angry.

Line 75 is from (*b*).
Line 77 (*b*) reads 'Subrání riár rakhí.'
Line 79 from (*b*) (*a*) reads:

Turká*n* mughalá*n* giptha.

Between lines 72 and 80 (*b*) inserts

Ganje*n* ispahá*n* phár bí*th*a

the meaning of which is not clear. Also after l. 81 (*b*) inserts,

Ba*kh*ta mír jane*gh*á khushtha
Dost o ispahána bo*kh*tha,

which is equally unintelligible.
Line 99. For pha 'towards' (*b*) reads phalav 'direction.'
Line 100. From (b) (*a*) reads:

Khosárá dehá*n* dírená
'Swiftly to his distant country.'

IV.

The Rise of the War between the Rinds and Lashárís.

[This poem is another fragment of the Chákar cycle, giving an account of the spoiling of Gohar's camels by the Lashárís, and Chákars' vow of revenge. The episode of the refugee-lizard is quoted by one of the characters as an illustration of the extreme Baloch doctrine of hospitality. Rehan and Járo the Rind warriors mentioned were sister's sons to Chákar. Dodá who is mentioned at the end is Dodá Gorgez, celebrated for the revenge he took for the spoiling of Sammí's cattle.]

No*dh* Bahrám gushí: jare*n* Rashkání Baloch gushí: imar Bulmat Kalmat karákuṭá*n* gushi: bá*gh*ár báutiá*n* gushí.

Whazh-gushe*n* Lorí biyár wa*th*í shá*gh*ár
Má sará chare*n* bairame phá*gh*ár
Jawá*n* mard dátárá gire dá*dh*á
Zí azh Sanniá giyáfená
Laḍi*th*a durre*n* Gohará sho*dh*á
*Akh*tha*gh*á bautí gwara Mírá
Chákurá shírá zí gawar-zírá
Gohará durrená hawar dá*th*a
"Bagavo Mílahá avan dáne*n*
Go má Láshárí jherave máne*n*"
Gohará laḍe sar-jama*gh* dáshtha
Dastá Gohar ma*n* Kacharak nyástha

Raptha*gh*ant Shoráná phare sailá
Chakurá Mírí bandane shahrá.
"Má tháshú*n* da*n* ba*gh*chae*n* Gájá
Gohar ḍáchí ma beghavá*n* danzent
Mái*gh*á shír da*n* náfa*ghán* shanzant"
Chákurá phurs' azh Malave*n* jatá,
"Zí*th* khan jat, de maná*n* hálá,
Cho khu*th*a khai go Gohara málá?"
Cho jawáb dá*th*a Melave*n* jatá,
"A*kh*tha*gh*á Láshárí hame chindrí
Khushtha*gh*á hir cho khena*gh*á mardí
Chham ja*th*a durrgoshe*n* Maheríyá
'Jat, hame gálá bile sheríyá
Phuṭure*n* Rind ma deravá*n* druáh ant
Ḍáchí pha hirá*n* hardame záhant'"
Ba*dh* burtha Reháná Nawávená
Phuzh Járavá jaur-jawávená
"Má phara durre*n* Gohará hirá*n*
Havbará shámálo janú*n* shirá*n*
Shart khanú*n* haisí chotavá birá*n*"
Bágar Jatoí jawáb dá*th*a
"Ba-khú-á*n* durren Gohara Sammí
Hota pha báutá*n* niya*th* khamí.
Shah Hussain cheravá roshá
Bibarí pheshá nishtha ma lo*gh*á.
Dar-shu*th*a bá*gh*ár azha gedá
Choravá*n* ilgá bo*kh*tha pha dínia (or pha randá)
Gur-khanána da*n* me*dh*ira lo*gh*á;
Demá dar-khaptha mardume jawáne*n*
Sharr kalánch ant cho dushtha*ghe*n shírá
Dholant oshíshe karáiyá*n*.
Kiámahá minnate khu*th*a-í báze*n*
'Choravá*n*, bá*gh*ár bil, maní shámen
I-katar márá phar wa*th*í náme*n*'
Na-jáne*n* joraejave*n* jatá*n*
Kálihá*n* bá*gh*ár khushtha pha latá*n*
O*dh* niya' lo*gh*á Sammave*n* sálo
Dast kauliyá phijatha dá*n*hí
'A*gh* phara bá*gh*árá na-ro bái
Ma*n* thai bhen, tho maní bhái'
Hot mirání dará á*kh*tha
Súrihá pha demá jawáb dá*th*a

'No Amul-máí*n*, no Amul-máí*n*!
Yarbare bosht, gal mayá goná.
Ma*n* phara bá*gh*ára khaná*n* choná
Án di*gh*ár shahmí bí*th* azh honá
Shingurá shast shángurá phanjáh
Drust pha bá*gh*ára bítha*gh*á yag-jáh
Omará nashke ishtha pha kaulá
Hon gire Bálácha phara honá
Súrih Dodá phara go*khán*.

Translation.

No*dh* son of Bahrám sings: to the fierce Rashkání Baloches he sings: of the war between the Bulmats and Kalmats, of the lizard becoming a refugee he sings.

Sweet singing minstrel bring your guitar, bind a large pagrí on your head, let the good man receive gifts from the generous.

Yesterday thence out of fertile Sanní, marched the fair Gohar: she came for shelter to the Mír, to Chákar ever-victorious with the sword. Then spake fair Gohar "The Lashárís are set on quarrelling with me, they let not my camels remains in the Mílah pass."

He collected all Gohar's camp and goods and placed her in the valley of Kacharak. Then they (*i. e.* the Lashárís) came wandering to Shorán; to a town under Mír Chákar's rule (saying), "We will gallop (our mares) to grove-encircled Gáj; let Gohar's female camels mourn for their young in the evening; let the milk from their (unmilked) udders drip down to their navels.

Chákar asked Mela the camel-herd, "Quick, camel-herd give me tidings. Who dealt thus with Gohar's cattle?" The camel-herd Mela thus replied: "The Lashárís came down here in wrath, they slew the young camels as if with the anger of men. Gohar the fair camel owner hinted to me to be silent about it, saying, 'Herdsman, keep this matter quiet, let the true Rinds remain in peace, the female camels daily bear more young ones.'"

Then Rehan the Nawáb became angry, and Járo the Phuzh bitter in reply. "In exchange for fair Gohar's young camels we will take a sevenfold revenge with our swords, we will gamble with heads and hair and turbans." And Bágar Jatoí answered and said, "Where are the fair Gohar and Sammi (her sister)? When was a hero wanting to his refugees? As in Sháh Hussain's day of trouble, Bíbarí sat in front of her house.

A lizard dropped out of a dwarf-palm, and the boys pursued it, chasing it into the chief's house. Then the good woman came out in front to meet them, wearing beautiful ivory bracelets, white as fresh drawn milk, slipped on over her soft arms. She entreated and implored them saying, 'Boys, leave the lizard alone, it is my refugee. Do so much for me, for your own honour's sake.'

The boys, ignorant and boorish camel-herds, killed the lizard with sticks. Her husband and lord was not there. She sent a complaint to him by letter, saying, 'If you do not go and fight on account of this lizard I am your sister and you are my brother!' Hot returned to his home, and the hero thus answered back 'Hear Amul-máí*n*! hear Amul-máí*n*;' stay where you are, do not speak.

I will act in such a way about this lizard that the ground will be filled with blood, and corpses lying sixty on one side and fifty on the other, all collected into one place for the lizard's sake, as when Omar was released on his own promise, as when Bálách took his revenge for blood, or the hero Doda for the cattle.

V.

The Competition between the Poets Sobhá and Gáhí.

Part I. Sobha addresses Gáhí on the question of the La*gh*árí refugees with Jawának, and taunts his tribe on their modern origin.

[These four poems constitute a complete specimen of a kind of exercise not uncommon among Baloch poets. Sobha a Khosa and Gáhí a La*gh*árí draw comparisons between their tribes and chiefs, challenging each other's claim to have come in with the original settlers under Mír Chákar, and taunting each other with failing in the exercise of the cardinal Baloch virtue, hospitality to refugees. Relán the Ḍom minstrel is commission by each poet to learn the words of his song, and to carry it back, and recite it in the assembly of the hostile tribe. The La*gh*árís and Khosas are old enemies, and their hostility still smoulders after thirty years of British rule.]

Sobha The*gh* Alí gushí: Jarwáre*n* Baloch, gushí: Khosagh Kaloí karákuṭá gushí: La*gh*árí báutiyá*n* kharde gál gushí:

Whazh-gushe*n* Reláná shá*dh*ihání shá*gh*á bare
Maí*n* salámá bi sháire*n* Gáhiyá diye
Nishtho dro*gh*ání zawáná wash khane,
Ewakhí será go maná*n* chachho*n* ṭule?
Bhúcharí Dálán kilát nám gire
Nuh-mane*n* bárá*n*rá wa*th*ár ka*n*s diye
Jawának urḍání ra*gh*azá roshe khafe

*Kh*i*n* shar háthí ra*gh*asá chít ártha*gh*e
Sher chápulá azh Kharṛá thalá guze
Go manán hair bí, zamíná jáhí lahe
Phesh guḍá maí*n* sailavání depá*n*thave
A*gh* thará wahm bí zamíná jáiz khane
Dav-chare*n* zahmání ná-washe*n* jáhá rase
'Shingura 'shángur lashkará*n* dem-o-dem khu*th*e
Zahrane*n* mardá*n* no*dh*-dilá seráfá ja*th*e.
Jawának uṛdání taware*n* goshá*n* khafí
Har-chyár demá ghoṛavání ḍáṭo ru*dh*í
Cho thaí bachhání dafání gonáf hushí
No*dh*í berána beghavá biyáyan thánahí.
Biyá, O Lashárí, azh gwareyá dar-khaptha*gh*e?
Guḍe Zunuwá ghoṛavá roshá gár a*th*e
Sailaí Míre*n* Chákurá phauzhá*n* rutha*gh*e
Rind nar-borá*n* azh zamíná resintha*gh*e
Khushtha*gh*á Rámen damámo charentha*gh*e.
Dai maná*n* nashká*n* tho ki*th*á*n* rosh khard bí*th*a*gh*e,
Bakar O Rámení ki*th*á*n* laḍá gon a*th*e?
Ghoṛavo uṛdá*n* phela*th*o Turkání ru*kh* a*th*
Doshí ma Jhalá Turk ghoṛáyá*n* granda*gh*á
An demá Gandáva*gh* Hu*dh*á mai*n* dem bí*th*a*gh*á
Turká*n* shád kámá Rind 'shame*dh*á zahr giptha*gh*ant
Hon azh chamání chimáká dar-khaptha*gh*ant
Gwashtha Nayániyá 'Mai*n* hu*dh*ábund go-khaptha*gh*ant.'
Lajavo, Shoráni dhaníyá*n* grán bi*th*a*gh*ant
Bijar, Phuzh, Chákar Shah*dh*ár á*kh*tha*gh*ant
Allan o Miskání Sahák Mádán a*th*ant
Bagavo lajjání sará katár dá*th*a*gh*ant
Asp go sonáe*n* zaríyá bashká*th*a*gh*ant
Rind azh no*kh*-zene*n* bihána er-khaptha*gh*ant
Piyá*dh*a*gh*á Rind azh ta*kh*t Shoráná á*kh*tha*gh*ant
Thorave Rindára olí Láshárí war a*dh*
Mir go Phulá azh Kawará drikhentha*gh*ant.
Whazh-ghushe*n* Relán shá*dh*ihání shá*gh*ár bizír
Mard pha báutá*n* choshaut, sardáre maní
Gáhwar o Háne*n* Sáhibáná jag-sahí
Gwar Nawáv Hán kúk burtha báze*n* barí
Gorisháníyá sángat o Káhan Marrí
Burzá go Summenzáiyá brá*dh*argarí
*Kh*tha gwar Háne*n* Jawánaká báutá*n* thaí
'Khosa*gh*á*n*, ki ma*n* neyá*n* La*gh*árí kha*dh*í'
Go má chyár sálá nishtha*gh*á báutí sharí*kh*

Bandave khohen nashkato hapt phushtí guzí
Mánik lo*gh*á har-khase ome*dh*á duráh
Mánik kaṭo bihisht jo sará
Gudí sammá, kotái pahráe pha*dh*á
Do Balochání á*kh*tha*gh*ant wákyái sará
Do shafá*n* bí*th*a gwar theí kháne*n* Me*th*irá.
Chham aṇzíyá*n* raptha*gh*ant gríhána pha*dh*á
Dobahá dá*th*en markhave, paidáish khu*th*e*n*
Lajjí bánukhá*n* phar wathí shána bashka*th*e*n*
Doda theí námúz ma*n* jihána mashhar a*th*e*n*
Guḍá dráhíye basthaí go Háne*n* Shakalá
Túmí gwá*dh*entha wa ganje*n* Bakará
Jawának phauzhání sara Gájí barbará
Sháh máríyá gone*kh*á go shere*n* Haidará
Ní ki á*kh*tba da*n* Sirí Mitháwaná
Niyám*gh*í Zíhár maí*n* sharí*kh*á*n* har do sará
Jahl-burziyá hek-byá resintha jará*n*
Deúní rebá er-khafí jáhíyá buná
Sher ki gwámesh phrushí loṛhiyá dará
Bá*n*z ki símur*gh* jhaṭí*th* maidáná sará
Hánen Arziyá gwá*n*kh be ambráyá ja*th*á
Khosa*gh*á nál bastha gala*gh*á kurká khu*th*á
Laj whántkárá*n* phíl-a*th*í símur*gh*íá burtha
Ispar o savze*n* ńeza*gh*á*n* Bashkyá sáh khu*th*a
Háne*n* Dilshád mardiyá berá thara*th*a
Shái phi*th*a ashk e*n* ki shawár paidá khu*th*a
Har do uṛdání nyáma*gh*á sámí suhr khu*th*a
Dodá Háne*n* Jawánakár zí*th*e*n* hair khu*th*a.

Translation.

Sobha son of The*gh* Alí sings: to the Jarwár Baloches he sings: of the fight between the Khosas and Kalois he sings: of the La*gh*árí refugees he sings, as follows:

Sweet singing Relán take away your guitar from the assembly, give my salutation to the poet Gáhí (saying), Sit down and make clean your tongue from falsehoods. How can you weigh single *seers* against *maunds*. You mention the forts of Bhúcharí and Dálán, you are placing nine-maund weights upon yourself. In the face of Jawának's armies you will fall in a day, beneath that elephant's foot you will be crushed, beneath its blow you will pass away from the valley of Kharṛ. Make peace with me that your land and place may remain to you before you are again terrified by my sword. If you are anxious, then legalize (the possession of) your land, for when swords are biting you will be in an unpleasant place, when on this side and on that armies stand face to face, and angry men are satisfying their swords' hearts (with slaughter).

When the shout of Jawának's hosts falls upon your ears, and the dust of the horsemen rises on every side, so that the moisture of your sons' mouths dries up, and the cloud-like (mares) come gallopping (loose) to their stables in the evening.

Come O Lashárí, where did you originate from? You were missing on the day of Zunú's horsemen; did you reap (a harvest) of Mír Chákar's army? did you chase the Rind chargers (lit. male chestnuts) from the land? When Rámen was killed you played the drum. Give me your tokens (to show) when you became separate from us. Did you march away with Bakar or with Rámen? Did you accompany the horsemen or the army to meet the Turks? That night when the Turkish cavalry thundered in Jhal, or towards Gandáva when God was on our side, when the Turks rejoiced and the Rinds became angry; blood issued from their eyelids, and the women said "our lords have met them."

The rulers of Shorán became heavy with shame; Bijar, Phuzh, Chákar and Shah*dh*ár arrived there, Allan and Sahák Miskání were there; they gave a string of camels to ransom the shame-faced ones (*i. e.*, the women taken by the Turks), horses they gave and bright gold, the Rinds alighted from their newly-saddled fillies, and on foot (having given up their horses) the Rinds returned from the throne of Shorán. Formerly the Lashárís also showed kindness to the Rinds, when they let Mír (Chákar) gallop away from Kawar on Phul (the name of a mare belonging to No*dh*banda*gh*).

Sweet-singing Relán, take up your guitar of merry-makings, (and declare) what sort of man my chief is towards refugees. Gáhwar and the Chief Sáhib *Kh*án are the most trustworthy of men; many times did they complain to the Nawáb, that the Gurchanis had made a union with the Káhan Marrís, and a brotherhood with the upper Summenzais. Your refugees came to our chief Jawának, saying, "we are Khosas, we are no longer Le*gh*árís." Four years did they stay with us, sharing in our protection.

The marks of their dwelling on the hills shall remain till seven generations pass. In Mánik's house every one lived in great hope; (for this) Mánik (shall have) a dwelling on the streams of Paradise.

(To your chief), in his latter age after the stage of deceit (in his second childhood?) came two Baloch women seeking for refuge; two nights they stayed with your mighty lord. Tears fell from their eyes and they cried aloud. He gave them the mares for twice their value, he made a profit of it, to his own shame he gave them to the shame-faced women.

Doda your chief became celebrated in the world! Then he made an agreement with Shakal Khán, and made them pass on to Túmí and wealthy Bakar.

The helper of Jawának's armies is the Pír Gájí Barbar. The saint accompanies us, riding on a swift camel, with the lion-like Ali. Now that we are come into the Sirí and Mitháwan (names of torrents on the Deráját frontier). Zíhár is the arbitrator between the parties on both sides. Up and down did the two bulls pursue each other (*hek-byá* a Punjábí phrase). Let us deceive them that they may descend to a lower place. Just as a tiger strikes down a buffalo outside its hedge, or as a Símur*gh* strikes a hawk on the plain, so did the *Kh*án call Arzí and his companions. The Khosas shod their horses, the troop made a rattling. Your chiefs were ashamed, as when the Símur*gh* carries off an elephant. With shields and grey spears Bashkyá made a shade. Dilshád *Kh*án heroically encompassed them about, honour to the father who bore you! Between the two armies they made their graves red. Dodá then quickly made peace with Jawának *Kh*án.

Part II.—*Gahí replies, praising bravery and taunting Sobha with being a coward, and not a true Rind.*

Gáhí Gorish gushí: Kaloí gushí: Sobhár phasave dú*th* gushí.

Whazh-gushe*n* Relá*n* shá*dh*ihání shá*gh*á biyár
Kau*n*sh bángavá gwar maní bálá*dh*á bidár
Chambare sak jan, malgí ḍílá *gh*am guzár
Jangí katárá dil machande: jawáná*n* bisár
Nishtha*gh*e satá whash nish námú*dh*-ṭawár
Azh waliyání khashtha*gh*e rand o kissawá*n*
Hair pha*dh*á: ráj-há*n* rosh ant, jang syáhe*n* shaf ant,
Jang pha*dh*á mard o markhaván jawai*n* rosh nayant
Gáhware*n* hindí bingave*n* hotá*n* charant
Dhaurave*n* koṭání sawádá zel khanant
Chandeá*n* warná pha dafá gozá*n* janant
Jangavo ninja bí, pha*dh*á pahná*dh* girant
Bingave*n* hotání ra*gh*ámá ambráh nayant
Azh pha*dh*á guḍá nishtho amso*dh* warant
Go doe*n* dastá*n* sar o zááná janant
Jangání ḍahká har-chyár khundá*n* phirant
Gwadile*n* mar go ginda*gh*á goriyá trahant
*K*shikání káre*n* me*dh*áná ravant

Taukal beṛiyá dilár telánká diant
Malgí ḍílá pha zirih o zirih-phosh khanant
Kadahá*n* zahrená sharábí nosh-khanant
Ma sa*gh*áráni thafthaghe*n* jhorá*n* khafant
Gáhware*n* the*gh*á phar wa*th*í námú*dh* janant
Go wa*th*i khánen Me*th*irá miski zar ant.
——. Whazh-gushe*n* Relá*n* shá*dh*ihání shá*gh*á bare
Maí*n* salámạ́ bi sháire*n* Sobhár diye
Me*th*ira randá zír ki Bompurá khai e
Ma*n* dilá zán ki tho Khosaghá má*th*í brá*th* naye
Sov labá*n* nyáma*gh*í dárá*n* sushe
Armáná ! zánant azh sa*dh*en sálá*n* gwastha*gh*e
Hai ganno*kh* e hai.zha thána kistha*gh*e
Bakar o Rámení sha*gh*ána mára jane
Tho khi*th*á*n* roshí Rind Lashárí bí*th*a*gh*e.
Ki ma*n* daryáyání lahravo chalán gár-a*th*e
Beghavá míre*n* Chákurá chaukídár a*th*e
Má wa*th*í shán cho masthare*n* Rindán phola*th*a
Ewakhí ser go maná*n* har-ro ṭola*th*a
Ma*n* thaí háthí ma*gh*azá shon diá*n*
Biyá me*dh*áná chambavá símur*gh* biá*n* janá*n*
Árava mardá*n* Sáwano lahrí rastha*gh*e
No*kh*-nochá*n* phá*gh* phi*th*í mardum bastha*gh*e
Mark násenthe, pha chihá*n* roshe shádehá
Shán phirenthe, ganda*gh*en gín dostehá
Ma*n* dilá zán ki maut thará nelí dá*n*sará
Dodáí dáng bí*th*en ma*n* bawre*n* chá*dh*ará
Me*dh* Máchíya Hamzahá jorí na be
Khosa*gh*á Rindá manavo máníya dare
Phuṭure*n* Rindá*n* cho khu*th*a báut pha*dh*á
Gohare hirání sara cho khu*th*a Míre*n* Chákurá
Sammíya go*kh*ání pha*dh*á Dodá lurá
Khoh sardemá kehare*n* máná lurá
Sar wa*th*í dá*th*aí garíme*n* mál sará.

Translation.

Gábí son of Gorish sings; the Kaloi sings; in reply to Sobhá he sings.

Sweet-singing Relán bring hither the guitar of rejoicings; bring into my life the fresh breeze of the morning; strike powerfully with your fingers, drive out grief from the bright (coloured) body. Do not frighten the heart with battle-array; praise heroes! Thou hast sat in the assembly with an ever sweet song of praise, and from our forefathers hast drawn forth our tracks and legends.

After greeting: The chief is the day, battle is black night; after a battle for men and horses there is no blessed day. The glittering weapons devour youthful warriors, and make populous forts empty of display. Some youths boast with their mouths, "We will be bold in the fight," but afterwards they turn their backs and are not in the company of the storm-cloud of young heroes. And afterwards they sit and lament and strike their heads and thighs with both hands.

At war's alarm they wander to all the four quarters. Cowardly men flee like wild asses, at mere sight (of a foe). The business of strong men is to go to the battle-field: they give their hearts a push off (from the shore) in the boat of confidence: they clothe their bright bodies in helmets and armour: they drain cups of fiery spirits; with burning white brands they fall upon the crowds, they wield their glittering blades to their own fame; with their own Lord and Chief they become like a sweet odour.

Sweet-singing Relá*n*, take away your guitar of rejoicings; give my greeting to the poet Sobha, and say 'Examine the tracks of our Chiefs, and see who was at Bompur. Know in your heart that you are not whole brother to the Khosas. A venal awarder of victory, you will be burnt with wood. Wretched man! They know that you have past a hundred years, that you are either a fool or have abandoned your home. And in that you cast scorn at me regarding Bakar and Rámen, when was it that you became a Rind or a Lashárí?

For you were lost in the waves of the river's flood, you were Mír Chákar's attendant for your (daily) evening food, while we, like mighty Rinds, sought for glory and every day weighed our single seers against maunds. I will explain things to your elephant's brain. Come into the battle-field, and, becoming a Símur*gh*, I will strike you down with my talons, as in Sáwan (the rains) the torrent sweeps away the men of Áro. You bind on the new and fine pagri of other men; you are gasping in death, when can you have any pleasure? You have cast away honour and made yourself a friend of worthless life; know in your heart that at last death will not spare you. There was disgrace on your head in the matter of Dodá. Me*dh*s and Máchís are not fit companions for Hamzah. You are excluded from home and food with Khosas and Rinds. For how did the true Rinds act with regard to refugees? How did Mír Chákar act with regard to Gohar's young camels; and about Sammí's cattle, how acted Dodá with the sword? when, like a tiger on the mountain tops, sword in hand, he gave up his life to protect the cattle of the poor.

N. B.—Dodá here alluded to is Dodá Gorgez, a legendary hero, not the Dodá Kaloi mentioned in the former poem.

III.—*Sobha's rejoinder, going over the legendary adventures of the Rinds, and asking what share the Kalois took in them.*

Sobhá The*gh* Alí gushí : Jarwáre*n* Baloch gushí : Gáhíyá phasave dá*th* gushí.

Kádir námá har sawáhá yád khaná*n*
Sag-satáre*n* banda*gh*í ardáse maná*n*
Relání Lorí biyá hadísání durr-gehá*n*
Sáz-khane shá*gh*á gwash Balochání nugdahá*n*
Dáimá nyá*dh*e bí*th*e*n* go Sultání sará*n*
Rind o Láshárí ma buná brá*th*á*n* dáimá
Má khu*th*a Lashárí Baloch khaptha pha sha*gh*án
Mehna e zánki ro*th* Panjgúra dehá*n*
Kech Panjgúr kissavá*n* gosh dár ki gushá*n*
Má hawá*n* Rind ú*n*, azh Halabá phá*dh*-á*kh*tha*gh*ú*n*
Dubarán jangí go jazízá mán-á*kh*tha*gh*ú*n*
Dem rosh-ásán saríná er-khaptha*gh*ú*n*
Hamzaí aulád sobh rasúlá bashká*th*a*gh*-ú*n*
Hárí malhána ráhí sháh-dagá khaptha*gh*ú*n*
Ungurí dastá thíbare jangá giptha*gh*ú*n*
Pha Karím sáz kuzratá*n* sho*dh*á gwastha*gh*ú*n*
Shahr Istámbol go Imámá wa*th* char*th*a*gh*ú*n*
Ma Ja*gh*ína gwar Shams-dín Sháh á*kh*tha*gh*ú*n*
Sho*dh*á Hárína pha turá jangí khashtha*gh*ú*n*
Ungurí Kech Makuráná bahr bí*th*a*gh*ú*n*
Shahr Sístáná o khamáná bahr bí*th*a*gh*ú*n*
She*dh* pha demá má Baloch tálá bítha*gh*ú*n*.
She*dh* pha demá tho wa*th*í nashká*n* de manán :
Rind má*n* Kechá ; Kech thá*n* demá nishtha*gh*e ?
Chil o chyár halká*n* ; go khai laḍá gon-a*th*e ?
Ní ki laḍána khaurí sarhaddá á*kh*tha*gh*ú*n*
Las-Belá o Kalmatíyá gíwar-tha*gh*ún
Habb Báráná pha muvárik she-bí*th*a*gh*ú*n*
Peshá Núhání azh Nalíyá er-khaptha*gh*ant
Jistkání ma Gáj sibáf á*kh*tha*gh*ant
Lak Salárí Chándeh azh Káchá khapth*gh*ant
Rind Lashárí Narmukh rej bu*kh*tha*gh*ant

Rinde Ḍháḍará saríná er-khaptha*gh*ant
Láshár pha Gandáva*gh* saráerá bí*th*a*gh*ant
Jalikán Loí tho khi*th*án joá*n* bahr a*th*e ?
Gind ! nawá*n* Gáhí tho ra*dh*iyá gon khaptha*gh*e
Arna Hárín bastha*ghen* baldá*n* gon a*th*e
Tho hawán roshe be-mayárí á*kh*tha*gh*e
Sáhib rosh zurtha*ghen*, zará*n* ártha*gh*e
Sherá mán-dá*th*a pha do-bandá khard bí*th*a*gh*e
Zinda*gh* o druáhá má*n* di*gh*árá sar-bi*th*a*gh*e
Phurse Gáhíyá, tho chi maskífí zinda*gh*e
Waptha*ghen* mardání tafá*kh*á*n* go ma*n* gane ?
Tho go dah lo*gh*á á*kh*tho báut bí*th*a*gh*e
Hán míriyá pha barátá*n* chárí a*th*e
Túpak daste Umar Há*n* bashká*th*a*gh*e
Ma*n* dilá zán ki tho mazai*n* shán mat niye
Tho ráj áhan-e, án thaí sultání sar-ant
Gwar maní mírá á*kh*tho báut bí*th*a*gh*e
Har chyár khundá*n* har hamú Rájá*n* dí*th*a*gh*e
Kumbhí go*kh*ání shagháná mára jane
Khoh phísh-bure*n*, ambaráni sifat khane
Gwashtha*gh*á*n* gálá*n* Gáhí, tho saharál na be
Me*dh*irá randá zír pha Bompúrá kháyant
Mánika halká hon avo lajján ri*kh*t ha*gh*ant
Da*n* pha*dh*-o-pheshí che*dh*a*gh*í nashk oshtá*th*a*gh*ant.

Translation.

Sobha son of The*gh* 'Alí sings; to the Jarwár Baloches he sings; in answer to Gáhí he sings.

Every morning I remember the Creator's name, my trust is in the service of God.

Come, minstrel Relá*n* with your beautiful legends, play on your guitar, chant the praises of the Baloches. You have ever been a dweller with kings, Rinds and Lasháris from the first have ever been your brethren.

I who called the Lasháris Baloches am scorned by you. Know that the scorn will travel to the country of Panjgúr. Attend, then, while I tell you the stories of Kech and Panjgúr. We are those Rinds who arose from Ḥalab, and twice joined battle with the infidels. Setting our faces to the rising sun, we descended from the west; we are Hamza's offspring, the Prophet gave us victory. Leading our strings of camels, we pursued our way along the highroad. Coming in this direction we fought again, and by the might of the Merciful we passed on thence. At the town of

Istámbol we rode with the Imám himself; In Ja*gh*ín we met with Shams-u'd-dín Sháh.

Thence we rapidly drove out Hárín in fight. Hither Kech and Makrán we distributed, we divided the cities of Sístán by khamáns (*i. e.* bows, a bow representing a man's share). Henceforward we Baloches separated, henceforward do you give me information about your track. The Rinds were in Kech: in what part of Kech did you settle? There were forty-four settlements: with which camp were you? Now when marching on we arrived at the torrent boundary, at Las-Bela and Kalmatí we separated, and we settled in prosperity at Habb and Bárán. First the Nuhánís descended by the Nalí pass. The Jutkánís came to the running water of Gáj. The Chándehs descended from Kách by the Lak and Silárí passes. The Rinds and Lashárís pitched on the irrigated lands of Narmukh. The Rinds descended from the west to Ḍháḍar, the Lashárís came from above down to Gandáva. In Jáliká*n* and Loí what streams did you share in? Look! Gáhí, perhaps you were with us by mistake. Or perhaps when Hárín was defeated, you were among the captives. You came shamelessly on that day, when, having robbed Sáhib of life (lit. day), you carried off his wealth. Having attained the low-lands you separated into two parties, alive and well you lay down (hiding yourselves) on the ground. Ask (and find out), O Gáhí, in what disgrace you are living; will you compare with us the dreams of sleeping men? You came with ten wives (lit. houses) and became a refugee, you posted yourself on the look out for our Khán's charities; you received a gun as a gift from the hand of Umar Khán; know in your heart that you are not worthy of great honour: You are their chief, and he is overlord of your chieftainship, for you came to our chief and became a refugee, and it was seen by all the chiefs in all four directions. You taunt me about the cattle at Kumbhí? You are but a cutter of phísh on the hills. (The leaves of the phísh or *Chamærops ritchicana* are cut to make matting.) You extol servants (not chiefs) My song is sung Gáhí, though you may not understand it. Take up the tracks of the chiefs who came to Bompúr. In Mánik's village blood has been shamefully shed, and formerly and lately cairns have been erected in memory of the slain.

IV.—*Gáhí's final answer, following up the Rind legend, and taunting Sobha with cowardice.*

Gáhí Gorish guslu: Kaloíe*n* Baloch gushí: Sobhár phasave dá*th* gushí.

Biyá o Relán shá*dh*ihání
Sháh*gh*ází chárayání

Majlis jawánen sarání
Zír maní guftár-gálán
Bar gwar jang-dosten syálán
Band-bozh gálán dahena
Phasaván sar pha sarena
Gondalán serán manena
Bar dan Sobháen nighoshí
Olí guftárán shamoshí
Zírí randá phírukeghá
Bahr khant milká phitheghá
Chi gushán man sháirára
Dil-harífen sugharára
Khashí Rindání shagháná
Yád khan' olí jiháua
Gosh sobha mangihání
Daftárí e Khosaghání
Rand zurthe Makurání
Rind Láshár dehání
Rind Láshárí áwárá
Rafthaghant azh Kech shahrá
Ákhthaghant Hárín malána
Mulk mítáfá giráua
Bráth-yárí bahr-khanána
Bíthaghún bahr khamáná
Má ki Jatoí yagsar athún
Sím joá pha-do athún
Mulk shahrá nemagh athún
Roz bahr pha thír-dárán
Chyárakhe ma Ḍbáḍar athant
Sermá ma Khánpur athant
Hand ma Rej deh athant
E maní perá o rand-en
Phuturen Rindání hand-en
Nám ma rájáu buland-en
Agh thará itibár na-bítha
Khasá go chamán na-dítha
Khatte kuhne gwar niyáthen
Gawáh sháhid kadh niyáthen
Kissavání kissav-áthant
Har-khase 'shí hanchosh-athant
Man sáhíyán Sobha, káp káṭe
Ne pha rand perowáṭe

Sov drapá Jawánake*gh*á
Júfo jhaṭá wa*th*íyá
Dro*gh* bande záhiríyá
Rást gusha*gh* rást riwáh-e*n*
Dro*gh* pha ímáná khatá-e*n*
Ar pha guftáre taiyár be
She*dh*-demá gawáhíyá de,
Khatte márá khash phe-de,
Biyá, azh shairá*n* karár kha*n*,
Olí Rindá*n* pha-pha*dh*á kha*n*
Nínava*kh*ta kissavá kha*n*
Surpha*dh*ení pha-gwará kha*n*
Maí*n* hadísán ma*n* dilá kha*n*
Sobha khaptha*gh*e azh drikh-bálá*n*
Thaí ni*gh*wárí sher nálá*n*
Sunya thaí Túví ḍálá*n*
Zurthíyá jangá maníyá
Zulm-zorá sahibíyá
Phrushtha*gh*á be-rona*gh*íyá
Zurtha*gh*e mardá*n* gihená
Chandehá juhl-khena*gh*ená
Rúnghan Báḍor yárá*n*
Sanghar ládí mazárá*n*
Shán hilále*n* khohistáná !
Muhammad Hán druh-giháná
Zeb Buzdárá hilál-an
Shaddav o khes go khawáhá*n*
Nind-nyá*dh* gwar Umaráhá*n*.
Hál khárthá*n* há*n*skárí
Gwar maní Sardár Háná
Gwar má báutí ki á*kh*tha
Azh thaí jangá rahe*th*a
Rúnghan o Kanḍor Báḍor
Shángo Sanghar da*n* Siríyá
Band Báze*n* Bákharíyá
Ráj a*th*ant símán daríyá
Drust khá*kh*tha*gh*ant whazh-dilíyá
Gwánkh Le*gh*ár charíyá
Phurs, Sobha shairára
Su*gh*ar o lekhí wa*th*ára
Wházhá 'shí meh*dh*irára
Wházhá thaí dem ma shustaí

Lashkarán Jáme ma khushtaí
Shakula ber shamushte
Mangehí shair pha hisáv-ant
Gál pha uzhmár o kitáv-ant
Majlise ma meraván bant
Dan nighoshán nishthaghen sat
Ákhthaghen báut ki kháiyant
Gird sardárán gihená
Dostant cho chhamán doená
Azh bachh-bráthán bingoená.
Sh'á pha báután wathíyá
Lajj neshtha pha-phadhíyá
Bakhoen shwáí mangeho shán
Kadh na khant chho ma Balochán
Ákhthaghe lajján wathíyá
Khashthaghant gudr lavílán
Mál madí go galímán
Basth-khárthant maín vakílá
Azh thaí koṭá gaṛhená
Thaí mehdhirá dír-zánaghená
Dítha go chhamán doená
Gosh Sobha o niyází
Esh maní guftár-bází
Tho ki guftáre kahitha
Man dí pha goshán sunitha
Túpaka dánga ganitha
Chi ma sháná sar-ákhtha ?
Phurse' sardárá wathíyá
Jawánaká be-ámilená
Bakhmal o bor go khawáhán
Dáthaghen maín Umará Hán
Hán Balochána Nawáva
Nukarí bokhtha azh tháná
Dátha hoten Jawánakára
Pholathí olí ba-nindán
Bithaghe báut go Rindán
Khoh phish-buren nihengan'
Phish phara khohá shaghán nest.

Translation.

Gáhí, son of Gorish, sings to the Kaloi Baloches : in answer to Sobha he sings :

Come, O Relá*n*, to the assembly, king and hero of song; In this assembly of young chiefs, take my speech and song, carry them to our war-loving foes. With propriety utter these few (lit. ten) words, answers given categorically, (head on head). They are arrows, of which a ser weighs a maund. Take them to Sobha, that he may listen to them, and forget his former songs. He will, he says, take up the track of our ancestors, he will distribute the paternal inheritance; what shall I say to the poet, to the cunning poet? Let him give up mocking at the Rinds and remember the former world. Say, O brave Sobha, you are the bard of the Khosas; you took up the track in Makrán, the lands of the Rinds and Lashárís.

The Rinds and Lashárís together set out from the city of Kech. They marched upon Hárín, taking the land of the country and dividing it among the brotherhood. We divided it by bows (*i. e.* a share to every one armed with a khamán or bow). We and the Jatois were united. At the border stream we separated into two parts, town and country we divided into halves, distributing our substance by arrow-stems. One-fourth were in Dháḍar, we got our satisfaction in Khánpur, our dwelling was in an irrigated country. This is our track and trace, the abode of the true Rinds, a name exalted among chiefs. If you do not believe it, no one has seen it with his eyes, there are no ancient documents forthcoming, there were no witnesses to attest it, but there are tales upon tales, every one says that so it was.

I am right, Sobha, you are blind and deaf, nor is your footprint to be found on the track. Fear to speak of the victory of Jawának, take your bribe quickly, for you are manifestly inventing falsehoods. To tell the truth is the true custom; falsehood is a blot upon honour. If you are ready with a song, henceforth give your evidence, bring forth and show me your documents. Come! desist from any further poems, let alone the Rinds of bygone days, and tell stories of the present times. Surround yourself with men of understanding and lay to heart our traditions. Sobha, you have past the time for leaping and flying, your youth is under your feet, bare are the branches of your Túba-tree. You were carried away in battle with us, by the fury and force of our chief, you were broken ingloriously.

You were defeated by brave men, by the deeply-hating Chándyas, by our friends of the Rúnghan and Vidor torrents, by the mighty tigers of Sanghar. Honour to the faithful hill-country, to the perfectly-brave Muhammad Khán, jewel of the loyal Bozdárs, with silken turbans and garments, dwelling with Umar Khán.

A sure message I brought to our chief 'Those who have taken refuge with me, have ceased to be with you in war. The Rúnghan, Kandor and

Vidor territories, from Sunghar to the Sirí torrent, the Band Báz and Bákhar, who were outside your chief's territories, have all come of their own accord and mount at the call of the La*gh*árís.

Ask, O poet Sobha! reckon yourself up in your mind and call our chief 'Lord.' If our chief has not washed your face, then you did not kill Lashkarán and Jám. Have you forgotten the revenge taken for Shakul?

An account is kept of good poems, their words are enduring and are written in books, they are recited in the assembly and they remain firm in the (recollection of the) listeners. Whenever refugees have come or shall come to worthy chiefs, they are dearer to them than their two eyes or than young sons and brothers. You, for those who take refuge with you, have not given up shameful conduct for the future. Where is your great honour? No one does so among Baloches. You brought your disgrace upon yourselves (by the way you acted towards the refugees). They displayed anger and rage.

Their cattle and property had been seized by the enemy. Our vakíl (demanded them) and brought them back bound from your fort! Your far-seeing chief saw with both his eyes then! Listen Sobha and attend. This is all my song. The song that you sang I also have heard with my ears. I have counted your gun-barrels. What honour is left to you? Ask your own chief, the unworthy Jawának. Velvet and chestnut mares and silk did our chief Umar Khán give him. The Baloch Kháns and Chiefs unloosed their white mares from their stables and gave them to the valiant Jawának!

Ask of your forefathers how refugees fared with the Rinds. It is the phísh-cutters on the hills that are the tigers. There is no disgrace in cutting phísh on the hills.

VI.—*A love-song.*

(Said to be by Jám Durrak a Dombkí, a celebrated poet who lived in the reign of Nasír Khán of Kalát in the last half of the eighteenth century. He is said to have undergone great persecution from the Khán on account of his love for a lady of the zanána.)

O Samín be-phursá bihishtiye
Azh latífá nema*gh*á khaiye
Man gulá dema mail khu*th*e doshí
Bairamo ásí sár khu*th*o mátos
Bo azh brí*kh*á*n* raptha*gh*an whashe*n*
Hijr maná*n* momín janant pásá*n*
Cho kahíráni árave*n* ásá*n*
Be-karár-á*n* ma nemshafí pásá*n*

Pha whashí o dost hubbo iklás*án*
Zillat*án* sáhsáre deáe jáná
'Nah' na khan*án* pha dost pharmáná
Cho ispar*án* demp*án* maní jáne
Chábuk o chashm díd paikáne
Kahr amuláni girgire*n* názant
Dadame gár-ant dadame báz-ant
Nai*n* dafá gír ki gál khan*án* roshe*n*
Nai*n* man*án* kurzat mazál chosh-e*n*
Pha dafá mahlíjá dí ján áy*án*
Nishtho duá go haw*án* roshe
Wa hu*dh*á meṛh*án* ma*n* dilá shefí
Er-khafí dost azh thangave*n* tha*kh*tá
Biái ro*dh*ána cho chyárdahí máh*án*
Masaro*n* bí cho Akbare Sháh*án*
Guḍá azh durr-chíre*n* dafá phurs*án*
'O badhashkání grán bahá lále*n*
Mára thaí lo*gh*wáre*n* sare*n* sau*gh*an
Irmirí gon-khapto*n* annágáhí
Phar thaí sah*th* sakale*n* nyá*dh*á*n*
Hon bahá ban pha sakale*n* *kh*ulk*án*.'

Another Song by Jám Durrak.

Doshí dil-raváhe*n* jání
Sartáj o samand kháḍání
Gwashthom pha dafí phanání
Osá thau machar haivání
Gird-i árav*án* phirwání
Chandí áshk*án*rá ziyání
Kulfo phrushtha*gh*á*n* shakání
Ishk o mani*th*a hakání
Gwashthom ke*gh*a*dh*en sázárá
Durchíno hazár názárá
Phulkand o shakar guptárá
O hál i fakíre esh-an
Zirde azh phirá*dh*án resh-an
An ki málik dozdár-an
An azh munkir*án* bezár-an
Jám jámav*án* kháksár-an
Harzatá darúd kár-an

Sháhe*n* kirdagár ásár-an
Gwafshe nem-shafá*n* nál-an.

Translation.

The rain that un-asked for falls from Heaven comes from the direction of the beloved one. Last I met a love face to face. The lightning springs forth, it is my love that has awaked me. The scent of her locks has sweetly seized me. The pain of separation sharply stings me in the night-watches, I spring up like the flame of Kahír-wood *(Prosopis spicigera)*, I am without rest in the midnight watches, for the sweetness of meeting with my love. Give my body some breathing-space from pain, I will not say 'No' to my loves command, my body is as a shield stretched forth. Let my eyes be gladdened by the sight of my fair one, let the pain caused by my lady be a little appeased ; sometimes it disappears, sometimes it increases. I cannot use my mouth to speak by day, I have no strength, she is so strong, to come to meet and speak to her.

I sit and pray for that day : 'O God, be merciful, and incline your heart to me.' Let my love come down from her golden throne, let her come growing like the waxing moon on its fourteenth day, let her be in front of me, and I shall be king Akbar. Then I shall ask from her pearly mouth 'O priceless ruby like the ba*dh*ashk fruit, make me your husband, bound by oath, my heart has been irrevocably taken possession of, I will live for the sake of your jewel-like beauty, I will spend my blood for you, fairest of beings.'

Second Song.

Last night I saw my heart-enchanting love, the crown and ornament of women. I spoke to her with my lips and said 'Do not behave foolishly, like the moth flying round a flame, O bane of many lovers.' The locks of hesitation are burst open, I have obeyed the call of true love. I said to my beautiful love, 'O fair one of a thousand wiles and sweet sugared speech, this poor wretch's state is this, his heart is galled with his complaints, he who is a chief and true friend is apart and averse from the avaricious. The heart of Jám is covered with dust. It remains but to say bism'illáh in the divine presence, to remember the King and Creator, and to pray through the cold midnight.

Riddles, Proverbs, &c.

The Baloches are very fond of riddles, which are always in rhyme. They are of a primitive type and generally defy solution. The more far-fetched they are, the more appreciated. Those first given are by Bráhim a Shambání who died about two years ago. He was celebrated for his riddles as well as for more serious compositions.

1. *Bujhárat.*—Ya shai jawai*n* ulkahá astá
Duzhmaneá resentha-ish khashtha
Bánghavá pahre ráh sará gwastha
Go minnat meṛhá*n* niya*dh* dastá
E bujhárat Bráhimá bastha.

Bozh. Warnái.

Riddle.—There was one good thing in the world; an enemy has pursued and turned it out. In the morning watch it passed along the road. Neither begging nor praying will bring it back again. Bráhim composed this riddle.

Answer.—Youth. (The enemy is old age.)

2. *Bujhárat.*—Hu*dh*ái kurzat o kárá
Zamín nesta*th* o di*gh*árá
Be khishtha*ghen* khishárá
Hu*dh*ái kurzat o kárá
Sabz o phul bahárá
Pha phasha*gh*á di taiyárá.

Riddle.—By God's might and power
With neither ground nor soil
Without a field being ploughed
By God's might and power
A green plant has flowered
And now its fruit is ripening.

Answer.—This was composed on seeing an ear of corn growing on the beam across the mouth of a well.

3. *Bujhárat.*—Bráhimá pairí gwashtha*gh*á gále
Dí*th*aghú*n* 'chíe rangá be hále
Range*n* kojhá andare*n* kále

Bozh.—Áskhohe.

Riddle.—Last year Brahim said 'I saw something of an indescribable sort. Its appearance was foul, but there was bright red within.

Answer.—A flint.

4. *Bujhárat.*—Ya shai jawai*n* ulkahá yaká
Go jherave jangá*n* sa*dh*bare saká
Har-khase kháí*th*, ja*th*í wa*th*í chaká
Ma*n* na gindání jagahe dhakká
Gosh dánábá shára bozh wa hakka

Bozh.—Chhá*th*.

Riddle.—There is one good thing in the world, a thousand times attacked with disputes and quarrels; every one comes and throws it over himself, yet I cannot see anywhere a sign of hurt. Let the wise ear attened and guess it right.

Answer.—A well.

5. *Bujhárat.*—Ya drashke jorentha páken hu*dh*áyá
Ma zamín phushtá pha jinde*n* razáyá
Bund yaken-í lámb-eṉ duáyá
Yake re*kh* bí*th*a, yake sawáyá

God has planted a tree, of itself it has grown up on the face of the earth; the root is one, the branches two; one is dust, the other ashes.

Answer.—The tree is mankind, the branches Musalmáns and Hindús.

6. Talabí naukarant kharde ajab bhat
Kadam pha lekhav-ant-ish kár o khidmat
Hame fauj dhurá be hathyár e*n*
Phi*th*í phoshinda*gh*á*n* yák o ṭawár e*n*
Hamo*dh*á lashkar khosh o khushár e*n*

A few servants of strange forms
They step by calculation on duty and service
They are an army bare and unarmed
Moving at the voice and call of other men
And there the army meet death and slaughter.

Answer.—The pieces at chess.

7. Nishtho dí*th*om pha na*dh*ar
*Á**n*** shahr be sáh watan
Ahání a*dh* jang o jadal
Nyámjí nawant yake dígar.

Sitting I saw with my sight
A city and masterless country.
There was war and strife between them
And no umpire betwixt the one and the other.

Answer.—A game at chaupar.

8. Wiláyat thars-e*n*, dost bar-karár-e*n*
Rava*gh*á gohár kisánake*n* taiyár-e*n*
Na ro*th*í má*th*, bachh olá sawár-e*n*
Phi*th* nestení, phíruk haiyát-e*n*

The country (in) fear, the mistress in comfort
The little sister ready to start
The mother will not move, the son is already mounted,
The father does not exist, the grandfather is alive.

Answer.

The above contains a series of puns on the names of a family, partly, in Sindhí. The name of the country Ḍáḍar contains in the last syllable 'ḍar' the allusion to fear. The name of the mistress Begam, read as 'be-*gh*am,' is the equivalent of 'bar-karár.' The sister's name is Haurí, the mother's Gaurí, meaning in Sindhí light and heavy. The son's name Sháh-sawár, the fathers *Gh*áibí, and the grandfather's Haiyát explain themselves.

9. Hu*dh*á pakko kuzraten bandá pálí*th*
Rusúl Muhammad e*n* ummatwálí
Hazáre*n* banda*gh* yaken thálí
Chamo*dh*á khas no ro*th* horg o khálí
Hamo*dh*á giptho harchí dí wártha-ish
Hamá whán zurtho lo*gh*á dí ártha-ish
Guḍá ja*th*o bhorentho thálí ujártha-ish

After an invocation to God and the prophet—
There are a thousand men to one dish,
No one goes thence empty-handed
There they take and eat everything
They take up the dish and carry it home,
And having thrown it down and broken it they leave it bare.

Answer.—This contains a pun on thálí, which means the hedge round a threshing-floor as well as a dish. After every one has carried away the corn he wants, the hedge also is torn down and carried away.

10. Dá*n*ki sháhá parware*n* khaptha ma*n* lo*gh* buná
Ní ki banda*ghán* razentha bí*th*a pha husn o phará*n*
Wash hadí*th* o khush lisán
Ro*th* go phule*n* ambalá*n*

As long as God had charge of him he lay at home ;
Now that men have constructed him he has become fresh and fair.
With sweet discourse and pleasant speech
He walks about with his fair companions.

Answer.—A man with a wooden leg.

11. Pyáláe phure*n* dí*th*a májái
Nishtha*gh*á lálo nesta*th*í dái
Pyáláe wártho lál shahíd bí*th*a
Chonán ki kulle*n* álímá dí*th*a

I saw a cup in a certain place
A bright one sat down without an attendant
This ruby like one drank up the cup, and then died
So that all men saw it.

Answer.—The flame of an oil-lamp which goes out after having drunk up the oil.

12. Do gohárá*n* dí*th*a ambází
Ajab khush ant gwar ambází
Naini suratá khamí
Yake khor dígar chamí

I saw two sisters embracing
Very happy at the embrace
There is not the slightest difference in their appearance
One is blind and the other has eyes.

Answer.—The reflection in a mirror.

13. Phairí khá*kh*tá*n* pha gi*dh*ár
Ma*n* Bakri shahr gwara
Bolí a*th*í washe*n* ṭawár
Dastá*n* gipthí nar-mazár.

Yesterday as I passed along the road
In the town of Bakkar
I heard a very sweet voice
But when I seized it, it was a fierce tiger.

Answer.—A snake.

14. *Proverbial sayings.*

Kahne litir o phíre*n* zál
Warná sará sár-bár.
Old shoes and an old wife
Are the burden of a young man's life.

Savze*n* cho hí*th*en, charpí cho meshí dumba*gh*á*n*.
As green as young corn, as fat as long-tailed sheep.
This saying refers to the Gwar or wild pistachio (*Pistacia khinjuk*).

Khaṭán so*kh*tha áfá phúkí wárth.
One burnt by hot milk will not drink even water without blowing on it.

This corresponds with the Hindustání proverb 'Dúdh ká jalyá chánchh hí píwat phúnk,' or the English. 'A burnt child dreads the fire.'

Málá sar-dai várá dosh.
Let the cattle go and milk the hedge.

This answers to 'Penny wise and pound foolish.'

ERRATA.

Page 3, line 8, *read* ز̂ *for* ز

„ 5, „ 33, „ pronounced *for* pronounced.

„ 7, „ 9, „ nyán̲wán̲ *for* nyán̲wán.

„ 7, „ 40, „ rasída *for* rasúda.

„ 8, „ 19, „ na*dh*ar *for* na*dh*ra.

„ 10, „ 2, *add* and jawarah *after* zik.

„ 13, „ 18, *read* phalo *for* phale.

„ 13, „ 29, „ límú, a „ límúa,

„ 16, „ 33, „ shá*kh*á „ shákhá.

„ 17, „ 8, „ marde „ mardá.

„ 24, „ 18, „ ki*th*án̲, thán̲ *for* ki*th*án̲ thán̲.

„ 25, „ 35, „ biyár *for* riyár.

„ 32, „ 14, „ see it himself *for* see himself.

„ 33, „ 38, *transpose* { nowhere hizhgarnen̲. / elsewhere thíhandá.

„ 37, „ 25, *read* welcome *for* welceme.

„ 42, „ 20, „ phạ*dh-ágh* *for* Pá*dh-ágh*.

„ 43, „ 24, „ bilí *for* kilí.

„ 44, „ 7, „ amnám *for* annám.

„ 44, „ 10-14, „ án̲— „ an̲—

„ 46, „ 16, „ leeward „ lee-ward.

„ 47, „ 12, „ باكي bákí „ باقي báqí.

„ 47, „ 34, „ baṭerá „ baterá.

„ 49, „ 5, „ bara*gh* „ bera*gh*.

„ 49, „ 10, *dele* P. burú, Skr. bhrú.

„ 49, „ 10, *after* برويث baroe*th* *add* بروان barwán, s. the eye-brow. P. burú, Skr. bhrú.

„ 54, „ 13, *read* pan̲war *for* panwar.

„ 57, „ 4, „ phashk „ phaskk.

„ 64, „ 21, *add* cf. Pashto jowal *after* to chew.

„ 66, „ 23, *read* oxen, mate *for* oxen mate.

„ 66, „ 27, *add* Pashto *after* joru.

„ 67, „ 9, „ P. „ world.

„ 71, „ 25, *read* dá*gh* *for* dágh.

„ 72, „ 33, „ tear „ burst.

Page 74, line 12, „ dára*gh* *for* dáragh.

„ 85, „ 20, „ sará sá „ sará sa.

„ 87, „ 32, „ sumb „ samb.

„ 93, „ 13, „ Maurorum *for* Mauroram.

„ 95, „ 13, „ sixtieth „ sixth.

„ 98, „ 10, „ khambar. Kambar *for* khambar—kambar.

„ 105, „ 13, „ گرانڈ *for* گراند

„ 105, „ 31, „ giryán „ girgán.

„ 108, „ 21, *after* گوانکهه gwáṉkh *insert* گونيچ gwánech, a camel driver.

„ 108, „ 33, *read* گوذان *for* گوزان

„ 109, „ 26, „ flesh „ fiesh.

„ 110, „ 3, „ گوماڈ „ گوماد

„ 110, „ 34, *after* گيانچ giánch *insert* گياف giyáf, fertile, extensive.

„ 111, „ 2, *read* Salix *for* Salia.

„ 114, „ 24, „ ma*n* „ ma*u*.

„ 115, „ 16, „ mán-dea*gh* *for* man-ḍea*gh*.

„ 115, „ 27, „ máhkání „ mahkání.

„ 117, „ 21, „ leap. „ leap !

„ 119, „ 31, „ mahisk „ mahis*k*.

„ 124, „ 30, „ نيغا ne*gh*á „ نيغار ne*gh*ár.

„ 124, „ 31, „ níkah „ nekah.

„ 125, „ 8, „ vakhtá „ vakhat.

„ 125, „ 16, „ P. *kh*wája „ P. *kh*waja.

„ 127, „ 6, *after* وهان whán *insert* وهانتكار whántkár, master, owner.

„ 127, „ 26, *read* عباسي *for* عبابي

„ 129, „ 33, *after* هليني halení *insert* همار himár, tender, delicate, beautiful.